THE MEMOIRS
OF
A PUBLISHER

The MEMOIRS of a PUBLISHER

by F. N. Doubleday

DOUBLEDAY & COMPANY, INC.

GARDEN CITY, NEW YORK

1972

Several passages of this book were privately printed in 1928 and 1929 as *A Few Indiscreet Recollections* and *More Indiscreet Recollections.*

Personal letters from Rudyard Kipling to F. N. Doubleday used by permission of A. P. Watt & Son.

Personal letters from Booth Tarkington to F. N. Doubleday used by permission of Brandt & Brandt.

Personal letters from T. E. Lawrence to F. N. Doubleday used by permission of Jonathan Cape, Limited.

"Effendi," by Christopher Morley, used by permission of *Saturday Review.* Copyright 1934 The Saturday Review Company, Inc.; renewed 1962 Saturday Review, Inc.

DESIGNED BY EARL TIDWELL
CALLIGRAPHY BY PAUL BACON
ART DIRECTION BY ALEX GOTFRYD

Library of Congress Catalog Card Number 72–76155
Copyright © 1972 by Nelson Doubleday
All Rights Reserved
Printed in the United States of America
First Edition

A NOTE

FRANK NELSON DOUBLEDAY disposed of all introductions in his Preface—so it is with some temerity that I dare to add a word to his book. He had a way of demolishing introductions, apologies, prefaces, and pretense in a few words. What, then, to call this? Perhaps "A Note" is enough.

My grandfather wrote this book for his immediate family. It was called *The Secret Memoirs of a Publisher,* and was for our eyes only. It was never published in its entirety. We do not think that now, by allowing this book to be read by others, we are violating his confidence. I suspect that, like all authors, he wrote to be read. So we are publishing it in our seventy-fifth year, principally and especially for those people of Doubleday who have become part of the extended family he created when he first set up shop.

And we think that his little book might be of interest, too, to that larger group of authors, fellow publishers, booksellers, librarians, agents, reviewers, friends, and readers generally who form the worldwide family of books. It is, after all, such people who liven our lives as publishers. We are happy to share this personal history with some of them.

"Effendi's" manuscript has been lightly and slightly edited, as he would have preferred. The chips, then, tend to fall where they may, for he always seemed to know what he wanted to say and he said it. A few footnotes, for identification and clarification, have been added.

Much of what my grandfather wrote in this memoir applies to Doubleday publishing today. At least we like to think so—and we all work to carry on in the tradition he began.

NELSON DOUBLEDAY

New York, 1972

CONTENTS

INTRODUCTION

An introduction is always included in a book of this kind, as I understand it, to give credit to a lot of people and usually to end by forgetting the most important.

Florence* induced me to write this autobiography against my will, and upon her head be all the blame. There are fifteen or twenty other people to whom I should like to give credit, but I would not undertake to pick out fifteen or twenty friends who would cover the list precisely—I would no doubt omit some and give myself a lot of trouble.

I have had in my life the most extraordinary and beautiful friendships, and it would be nothing short of presumptuous for me to attempt to acknowledge individually my indebtedness to these friends. Perhaps if I live to be ninety or a hundred, I shall learn how to do it, in which case I will let you know.

F.N.D.

* Florence Doubleday, the second wife of Frank Nelson Doubleday.

PREFACE

EVERY BOOK that does not amount to anything has a preface and an introduction. It seems to be a convention and I suppose it is valuable, because it makes the book less severe and dull if there are a few half-filled pages at the beginning.

Another use of the preface is to assure the reader that, no matter how egotistical one seems, one is really modesty itself. This is a difficult task when anyone writes an autobiography; I cannot imagine a more self-centered affair.

This manuscript was written during a period of illness and the work helped the author through many hours of discomfort. It has been entirely composed in an automobile, which offers relief for nervous chills and feelings much appreciated by the "chillee."

I have no very convincing argument to offer as to the innate modesty of this record, but as long as it does not get spread about very much, it ought not to ruin my reputation.

F.N.D.

December 1926

THE MEMOIRS
OF
A PUBLISHER

CHAPTER I

EIGHTEEN YEARS
WITH SCRIBNER'S

EARLY DAYS

ONE DAY my mother was riding in a Brooklyn horse car when a boy got in and delivered a circular to each passenger. At that time General Custer had just been killed by Sitting Bull. The circular contained a picture of an Indian, with the words:

> Above you see the portrait of Sitting Bull, the murderer of General Custer, and below you find the address of

F. N. DOUBLEDAY
Book and Job Printer
106 First Place
Brooklyn, N.Y.

My mother was horrified. I was about ten or twelve years old. I have often thought of Nelson's daring advertising* and wondered if it did not have its beginning then.

That is where printer's ink first let its poison into my

---

* Nelson Doubleday, F.N.D.'s son, pioneered many modern book mail-order techniques.

[1]

blood. I had saved up fifteen dollars, bought a printing press, and worked up quite a business, making about ten dollars a week printing all kinds of things, among them the worst visiting cards the world has ever seen, and hat tips to be pasted in straw hats. "Bon Ton" was one, for which I had an order for ten thousand. I printed them all "Bon Tom," but as the customer never noticed it, there was no trouble.

Gradually I employed some other boys, one of whom was Herbert Plimpton, my most intimate boyhood friend. He was one of those reliable fellows who always got up early in the morning, and I was one of the unreliable ones who never wakened until he was called. Because I had to go to school, the best time to run our printing establishment was between six and eight o'clock in the morning. I was incapable of getting up at six without great assistance, so I tied a string to my toe and let it hang out of the window, and at six o'clock Herbert would come and pull the string and force me to go to work.

It is extraordinary the number of things we did and the amount of money we made in those primitive times. I gradually improved my printing plant, and I remember distinctly the pride I felt when I had a press which inked itself, instead of the ink being put on the type by hand. My entire office consisted of a little box three feet high and two feet wide, which I subsequently gave to my brother Russell, who gave it to Florence, who has it now. It still shows signs of many-colored inks and fairly rough usage, but it was a clever little arrangement and answered every purpose for the whole printing business.

My experiences with this printing press gave me a love

of printer's ink and aroused in me an ambition to become a publisher. I knew that a publisher had to have two things, neither of which I possessed. One was a good education, another was sufficient capital. But the lack of these things did not distress me. I knew that I could get someone to work with me or for me who was well equipped for the literary side and on whose judgment I could rely. In a small way I was a reader myself, and always had an eye for a book that I thought would sell. On the whole, I think I managed this part of the business pretty well, considering that I had no real substance in the way of an education. If I had been more favored in this direction, I should no doubt have done very much better, but I will say that I did have the sense to seek advice and to act on it, so I got along pretty well.

When I was fourteen years old my father's hat business failed. I had not had more than two or three years of schooling altogether and had to go to work. But I was bound to be a publisher, and I went to New York and walked all over the town to find out which publisher I would go to, for I did not want to waste myself on a firm which would never amount to anything. I can perfectly well remember the awful cheek that I possessed. It seemed to me quite proper that I should take some trouble to find out who was the best publisher, instead of taking the first job I could get and finding, perhaps, that my opportunities were limited.

I finally decided on Scribner's as most worthy of my attention. They had a store fifty feet on Broadway and two hundred feet deep which I concluded was just the thing for me and I would get a job there.

So I worked up a letter of introduction from A. S. Barnes & Company, educational publishers, to Mr. J. Blair Scribner, which I presented and asked if he did not want to hire a boy. He said he did not—that he did not hire boys anyhow—that was Mr. Armstrong's business.

So I tackled Mr. Armstrong, whose desk was next to Mr. Scribner's, and asked him if he did not want to hire a boy. He said he did not need any.

"This is the fifteenth of December," I argued, "and you will need help over Christmas. I think you had better take me. It will cost you only three dollars a week."

He still resisted my blandishments and insisted that he did not need me; but I told him: "You will make a great mistake if you don't take me on. If you hire me, you will get a good boy."

"You seem to have a high opinion of yourself," he remarked.

"Yes," I replied, "I have. I only ask the chance to see if I can't get you to think as favorably of me as I do of myself."

"Well," said he, "you are so cheeky that I'll give you a job for a week."

I was there eighteen years.

The first job I had was carrying books, as many as twenty-five at a time, from the bindery to the packing room —a job which bored me so excessively that I finally worked my way up to the front of the store to surreptitiously become a salesman. A beautiful young lady named Miss Glenn, from Cleveland, a member of a very wealthy family, came into the store clad in expensive furs, and I noticed that she had no one to wait on her. I introduced myself by saying, "I have been on this job only half a day and I don't know much about books; but if you want any information, I can get it for you."

She replied that she did. The result was that she bought two hundred dollars' worth of books, and she used to come in nearly every day and buy anywhere from five to ten dollars' worth. She always asked for me, and I waited on her; and I tried to convince my boss in the rear of the store that I was much more valuable waiting on customers than carrying books.

After the Christmas season I was put in the manufacturing department and spent a year or two in that field. Mine was a dull assignment. Most of my time was occupied in copying out orders and checking bills, and I was very ambitious and anxious to get out of it, so I suggested to Mr. Scribner that he give me the job of advertising man. He told me to write a review and bring it to him, and he could judge by that if I could write a good advertisement. I very well remember that, like an idiot, I selected the *History of Christianity,* by Professor Fisher, and wrote a review of a book about which I knew nothing and had not the sense to dissemble. I gave it to Mr. Scribner to read, and he calmly remarked after a careful perusal that he had read many reviews and this was by far the worst of any.

I do not know why I got the job after that—I suppose that again pure cheek did it somehow. At all events, I got hold of the advertising for the fiction, and Mr. John Scribner kept the advertising for the religious books. We spent the appropriation twice over, and, as I remember, more than wrecked the advertising budget.

And again, Mr. John Scribner's job was taken away from him and given to me—why, I cannot now imagine. It must have been some curious fate which made it possible for these difficulties to be overcome—some power beyond anything that I possessed.

As time went on, I gradually improved my position until I became the editor of *The Book-Buyer.* There was one amusing experience in connection with this. I wanted a "Letter from England" for *The Book-Buyer,* which was a house organ affair, and I could not get anybody to write me one for nothing and Mr. Scribner thought we could not afford to pay for it. So I used to go down in the cellar where it was dark and write my own English letter every month.

One day Mr. Scribner found me down there and asked me what I was doing. I told him I was writing the English letter for *The Book-Buyer,* and trying to use the dark, damp atmosphere to get it in the right key. But I got too many extraordinary things in it, many of which were credited to our English partner, Mr. Charles Welford, who objected, and I was finally forced to abandon the idea of a regular English letter.

OUTSIDE JOBS

Among the many jobs of outside work which I undertook while employed by Charles Scribner's Sons in order to add to my small earnings was a connection with the New York *Times.* They ran once a week a literary column of *News and Notes,* conducted by a Boston clergyman. I thought it very poorly done. He would reprint the same paragraph several times, giving the same information, in what I considered a careless fashion. This seemed to me to be my chance, and I cut out the paragraphs which showed this duplication and poor management, pasted them on a piece of paper, and took them to John Foord, at that time the editor of the New York *Times.* I urged him to give me the job of preparing this weekly column of *News and Notes,* and promised that it should contain accurate information and real news. I also wanted the job of writing some book reviews.

He did not seem enthusiastic, but told me that if I would write a book review and send it to him he would consider the matter—if he could give me a job, he would print the review; but if he did not print the review, I might know that he had no job for me.

I remember that I took an English book on Bartolozzi, the Italian engraver, as I was very much interested in old prints at that time. I sent this review to Mr. Foord, and confidently looked forward to its publication in the next week's paper. Much to my disappointment, it did not appear, nor the next week, nor the week after that. I had fully given up ever hearing of the subject again, when suddenly it was printed. I immediately applied for the job, which Mr. Foord gave me, and I conducted the column in the *Times* for a year or two.

My leaving the *Times* was a matter of great humiliation under the circumstances. I received a letter from Mr. Charles R. Miller, who succeeded John Foord as the editor of the paper. Mr. Miller wrote the worst hand of anybody I ever knew, and his letter was simply beyond me to decipher. I took it to a friend who could read anything, believing that I had received a letter of commendation, as my notes, I thought, had been very good of late. But my friend remarked, having looked at the note for a moment, "You're fired," which proved to be true.

Perhaps they were cutting down expenses, or perhaps my stuff was rot. I never found out which was the reason, but I had my own opinion.

I also did correspondence for the Boston *Advertiser* and the Boston *Courier,* all at night after my work at Scribner's was finished. I used to sit up pretty late doing these jobs and I don't suppose it did me any good.

After the *Times* episode Mr. Foord went to the Brooklyn *Union* as editor and proprietor, and I used to conduct a column of literary news and notes for that paper; but that it was not very good is sufficiently proved by the fact that Mr. Foord lost his fortune and lost the paper itself after six or eight months of effort to make it a success.

It was at this time that I first met Walter Hines Page, who had been employed by Mr. Foord as an editorial writer. He was just starting his career as an editor, having left a job in the South, and was trying to work his way into a good job in the North. We became fast friends at once— a friendship which lasted, as we all know, for many years.

JOHN I. BLAIR

Mr. Scribner had the most extraordinary grandfather I ever heard of in my life. He was over eighty years old, six feet three inches tall, weighed two hundred pounds, and carried a carpetbag that must have been a severe burden to tote around the country.

One day he came to me and said, "My son, do you ever tell a lie?"

I replied that I was not entirely deficient in the art.

"Let me give you a piece of advice," he said. "Whenever you lie, write it down on a piece of paper and keep a copy of it. Please copy this letter."

He was a great railroad man and owned a little railroad all by himself in New Jersey—the Blairstown Railroad,† I think it was called. He was also the proprietor of a large railroad in the West. One day he told me that he went into a restaurant in one of the stations on his railroad, and when he left he paid the cashier twenty-five cents for his luncheon.

The cashier called him back and said, "Here, we only give that rate to people who belong to the road."

"That's all right," the old man replied, "because the road belongs to me."

I always had some sympathy with another story that they tell of him, because my handwriting has been so difficult to decipher. He lived at Blairstown, which, if I remember rightly, is some sixty or seventy miles from New York, perhaps even more, and he conducted a general country store. Every week or so he would send a truck, drawn by horses, all the way to New York to buy supplies, giving the driver a list of the things that he was to purchase.

One week he was more careless than usual in writing out his order, and when the driver reached New York he could not read it. After puzzling over the matter for some time, he abandoned the idea of getting the supplies that Mr. Blair needed, and went all the way back to Blairstown empty-handed.

† Actually it was the Delaware, Lackawanna and Western. He was also part owner of the Union Pacific.

Mr. Blair was very much annoyed to find his order un-
filled, and asked what was the matter. The driver handed
him the order, and the old man said, "What's this! What's
this! I never saw such writing."

The driver replied, "That contains the instructions you
gave me to purchase goods in New York, but none of us
could read it."

When he knew what it was, the old man immediately
read every item without the slightest difficulty, and sent the
driver back again to New York.

Mr. Blair was a canny old gentleman, made a huge
amount of money, and I think was responsible, probably,
for the start of the Scribner fortune. He lived to be eighty-
five or more and died in his tracks—a wonderful personality.

CONDUCTING A THEOLOGICAL PERIODICAL

I had an interesting time with two great theologians: one,
Charles A. Briggs, and the other, Dr. James Patten. They
were both editors of the *Presbyterian Review,* and absolutely opposed in their theological attitudes. Briggs was a
liberal, and Patten was a Scotch Presbyterian of the deepest,
bluest dye. So far as I could see, each had authority to
close each issue of the magazine stressing his particular
editorial policy, and each maneuvered to put over that
policy. I could not see that anybody *except* these two people
cared anything at all about the editorial policy of the
magazine, so it didn't make much difference to me, and I
would close the magazine and "put it to bed," as going to
press was called in those days. Then one or the other would
come back and want to reopen it, and I would have a first-

class row to convince him that it was printed (when it was only on press). I think I told more theological lies in those days than in any one period of my life since.

CHARLES SCRIBNER ASCENDS THE THRONE

I had been with Scribner's only a few months when Mr. Blair Scribner died. He was a courteous gentleman and very friendly to me, whom he hardly knew. He acted as the head of the business, and was succeeded by the present president, Charles Scribner, who had little to do with the business before his brother's death.

Upon his succession the business took on new activity and power. He began by having a row with Armstrong, the junior partner of Scribner, Armstrong & Company, and succeeded in firing him out of the firm. We all disliked Armstrong, as a mean Scotsman, and we were glad to see him go. I think we all gloried in his misfortune.

Charles Scribner then took the business in both hands and made it increasingly valuable and profitable. I should like to devote about fifteen volumes to my experiences with Mr. Scribner, and publish them as an example to people whose tongues are too sharp. During most of the sixteen or eighteen years that I was with him I disliked exceedingly many of his qualities, and he had a power over me which was extraordinary. For instance, I would get up a scheme and work it out with the utmost care and enthusiasm, and take it to him for approval. His expressions of scorn and distaste were particularly hard to bear. I was so supersensitive that many times his criticism, or style of criticism, brought on active nausea, so that my schemes and my plans were lost in the distress of my stomach. Sometimes I would go back and suggest them over again in a different form. Many were the ideas that I gave up simply because I could not stand these strains.

I remember, for instance, the Law Library, which was not an original idea, but I had a different method of approach. He would have nothing to do with it, and made me feel like an idiot to have suggested it. This happened over and over again, and caused me to cherish the most unfriendly feeling, which was the most foolish thing I ever did. At the end of ten years, being a little slow, it suddenly occurred to me that I was poisoning myself and doing him no harm, much to my disappointment. I finally went to him and told him that I had disliked him for ten years, and I proposed to stop. He seemed extremely surprised and could not imagine why. At all events, it was the end of the feud, and ever since then we have soft-soaped each other as much as the traffic would bear.

Now that many years have passed over my head and I have known something of what sickness means, I remember that Mr. Scribner suffered extremely from sciatica, a most painful and exhausting disease. Perhaps many of my troubles with him might be attributed to that cause.

CHAPTER II

THE STORY OF
SCRIBNER'S MAGAZINE

In 1887 Mr. Scribner was permitted by his contract with the Century Company to start a new magazine and call it *Scribner's*. He had sold *Scribner's Magazine* to the Century Company in 1882, with the understanding that the word "Scribner" should not be used on a magazine for five years. In 1887 this period was up, and plans were formulated for the making of a new *Scribner's Magazine*. I was crazy to get into the game, but there seemed to be no way; apparently I had been entirely ignored in the planning of the magazine. The editor had been selected—Mr. E. L. Burlingame, a scholarly and fine gentleman who had about as much practical sense concerning the publication of a magazine to interest a large number of people as a Greek college professor. Mr. W. A. Paton, an old friend of Charles Scribner, was made business manager, and I stood on the sidelines and looked on.

The first number was to be published the fifteenth of December and dated January. Mr. Paton was a very jovial person and a member of many clubs. In those good old days one could get all one wanted to drink, and Mr. Paton soon got so much that he was incapacitated for carrying on the formation of the new magazine's organization. Along about November first he disappeared entirely one day, and Mr. Scribner asked if I thought I could run the job of business manager of *Scribner's Magazine*. With my natural modesty, I insisted that I could run it better than the former incumbent; so I became business manager of *Scribner's,* working with an editor in whom I did not believe and whose ideas were as different from mine as two sets of ideas could be.

But I had enough to occupy me to get the magazine ready for publication December fifteenth. I very well remember the day on which that number was brought out. It was cold and snowy, which we thought would injure the sale. Much to our surprise, the magazine sold like hotcakes, and in two weeks we did not have a copy.

Mr. Scribner was very anxious to print fifty thousand more of the February number, but in my opinion the February issue was, if possible, duller than the January, and I induced him to let me reduce the printing order.

It must be remembered that starting a new magazine was more of a literary event in those days than it is now. All the newspapers in the country had notices about this new magazine, with various comments, more or less intelligent. I was torn by conflicting emotions. I wanted to push the magazine as hard as I could and spend Mr. Scribner's money to get circulation, but I was positive that the material it contained would not have any large popular appeal and the money would be lost. I am sorry to say I was right, for a large proportion of the first issue came back to us from the News Company, even though we thought all the copies had been sold; and an even larger proportion of the second number. Mr. Burlingame's idea was to make a scholarly magazine, which I felt was interesting to what might be considered highbrows. It was very distinguished, but poorly illustrated from the point of view of any sensational interest.

The success of the *Century Magazine* had been brought about by the publication of the Civil War papers.* The circulation went up from seventy-five or eighty thousand to three hundred and twenty-five thousand, mostly sold on the newsstands at thirty-five cents. After the success of the war papers, the circulation was partly held by a brilliant series of articles on Lincoln, by Nicolay and Hay. This contained much new material and was very popular, and was later followed up by a series on Napoleon, by Sloane, with beautiful illustrations. But, like all ventures of this kind, the circulation steadily decreased, with a few spasmodic upward turns, until today I suppose it sells about twenty-five thousand.

In those degenerate days we thought that all we had to do to secure a circulation was to get some idea paralleling an idea run successfully by some other periodical; and because of the success of the Napoleon and Lincoln articles, Mr. Burlingame thought that all the new gossip about Julius Caesar would interest our readers. When we failed, because he discovered that Julius was not figuring often on the front pages of the newspapers, he tried the ancient

* A series of memoirs and recollections published in book form as *Battles and Leaders of the Civil War.*

[15]

Assyrians. But even the Assyrians did not appeal to the hoi-polloi; the magazine kept going lower and lower, and I was at my wit's end to know what to do. There was constant bickering between Mr. Burlingame's department and my own, and poor Mr. Scribner had to hear both sides. I think he felt that my side was the most profitable, but that Mr. Burlingame's idea was the most distinguished. The question, therefore, arose, how much money he would lose by making a distinguished magazine instead of what I wanted, which was a popular magazine. As usual, I had dozens of schemes which I presented to Mr. Burlingame, without convincing him of anything. To show you how rigid his ideas were—he declined to put at the end of a chapter of a serial the words, "Continued in the next number." He said that any intelligent person would know that a serial would be continued in the next number, and refused to pay any attention to this suggestion.

I also suggested that we should have a résumé of what had gone before in the serial, which I planned to spread about the country to get publicity. This he thought extremely vulgar and would not consider for a moment. As I remember, I was in his office about once a day with an idea, and I came out of his office with the same idea unfertilized. I can only remember two or three unimportant things that I ever suggested that he thought were worth anything.

The very first number of the magazine contained an article by William James. I cut out the first paragraph, which read:

> "Assuming the fundamental postulate of
> physiological psychology," etc., etc.

and pasted it in my hat, which I was very careful to leave around where Mr. Scribner would notice it. One day he asked: "What have you got pasted in your hat?" and I replied, "That is a sample of the kind of thing you expect me to sell one hundred and twenty-five thousand copies of each month."

He didn't know whether to be offended or amused; but nothing came of it, and we went on making a dull magazine, expecting to sell one hundred and twenty-five thousand and really getting rid of perhaps forty or fifty thousand at the most.

One day a man who gave his name as Harlow walked into my office and said that he was in a position to get fifty thousand subscribers to *Scribner's Magazine* if I cared to have them. I nearly kissed him, unattractive as he was. He was a tall, loose-jointed, unshaven, ill-dressed, down-at-the-heels-looking person in a dirty Prince Albert coat, with a hand like a gorilla's. He could take a four-volume set of books in his paw and entirely encompass it like a small box of candy.

I said that, notwithstanding his down-and-out look, if he could get us fifty thousand subscriptions, I would make his fortune for him.

"It's easy enough," he replied. "I will show you how it is to be done. You act the part of the customer, and I will be the agent and come into your office."

He went out of the door, and came in with a set of books held in his paw as I have described. He pushed it in front of my face and said, "Mr. Doubleday, I have come to present you with a very valuable four-volume set of books. It won't cost you a cent—all you have to do is to subscribe to *Scribner's Magazine* for a couple of years. The price is six dollars and it is worth at least twice as much."

I said, "Go out for a couple of hours and try that. I will have some blanks typewritten for you."

So I made up some blanks and gave him a set of Bourrienne's *Life of Napoleon* in four ordinary-sized volumes, which was the set he happened to pick up on my desk.

He was back in my office in a couple of hours with about ten orders, signed by very good people. We delivered these orders and collected the money, and this was the beginning, so far as I know, of that kind of installment subscription business. Within a year, if I remember rightly, we had sixty or seventy thousand paid subscriptions on this plan.

Of course, Harlow went dippy over his success and the large amount of money he made, and resigned in a huff to go to some other magazine and work the same plan, but he was never successful again. This installment plan of selling books with a magazine subscription was carried on during my tenure of office; we established branches all over the country and did a very large business. In those good old days, when collections were easier than they are now, we made a good profit.

SUBSCRIPTION BOOK SETS

One of the most important plans with which I was connected and which I carried out myself was the collection of standard authors for the subscription book business. As mentioned in the paragraph describing the start of *Scribner's Magazine,* we had a small subscription business by which we sold books in connection with a year's subscription, and I was promoted soon to be the manager of the whole subscription department.

The plan that I conceived was to get all the authors whose works were very important complete in Scribner's hands.

The first and most important one was Rudyard Kipling. In a separate chapter I wish to say something about my connection with Kipling, but this particular incident that I will relate now had most to do with the business side of the subscription department.

Edward Bok said to me one day, "Will you get me a complete set of Kipling in uniform binding?" I told him that it did not exist. That gave me an idea that perhaps I could get permission to make a uniform set. The difficulties of such a job, even now as I look back on it, were tremendous. Scribner's had no Kipling book at all on their list and no association with Kipling; the Century Company had three books, Macmillan eight, Appleton one, and I had to think of a good reason why they should give up to Scribner, who had no hold on Kipling, the right to publish a complete set.

I finally worked it out by trying to get Mr. Kipling's own help and enthusiasm. I figured that he would be the one who would make the money, or most of it. So I carefully thought out a plan to present the subject to him in the best way I could.

I began by putting it up to Mr. Scribner, who thought mighty little of the scheme. He said it was impossible that I should get three publishers to permit us to do such a thing. It did not seem impossible to me at all. He said it was not worth a railroad ticket to go to Brattleboro and see Mr. Kipling.

This completely upset me, but I finally came back and said, "It is worth a postage stamp, isn't it?" So I wrote to Mr. Kipling, asking if he could see me as representing Charles Scribner's Sons; I had an original plan to present to him.

I received a courteous reply, which is now with my Kipling letters, saying that, if I chose to make the long journey to Brattleboro in midwinter, he would be very happy to see me, but he could think of nothing which would pay me for my trouble.

This, I thought, was a fine beginning, and I arrived at Mr. Kipling's house, Naulahka, one cold snowy morning, and was received with the utmost cordiality. I at once unfolded my scheme, which interested Mr. and Mrs. Kipling very much. Kipling said, "It is a fine scheme, but you never can work it out."

"It is easy to work it out if you approve," I said, "because all of these publishers have got to please you; and if you ask them to do you a favor and they decline, they know that they would probably never get another contribution from you."

"Well," he said, "as far as I am concerned, I am very anxious to have the thing brought about, and I give you authority to represent me and see what you can do."

I told him that was all I wanted and when I had made more progress I would communicate with him. This was the first time I ever had anything to do with Mr. Kipling.

I returned at once to New York and went to see the Macmillan Company, and asked them if they would permit us to make an edition to be sold only in complete sets, and told them I would give them two thousand dollars (I think it was) for the privilege.

Mr. Brett† said that he saw no objection to it, but raised the price, I think, five hundred or a thousand dollars, and I accepted it. Thus with one fell swoop I had eight volumes of the set to start with.

I then went to Appleton and had no difficulty in getting the right for *Many Inventions,* which had not been particularly successful; but when I got to the Century Company, I felt as if I were in a den of wildcats. They were hurt, offended, grieved, that anybody should think of such a scheme, which, as a matter of fact, they said, they had thought of doing themselves years before. I asked if they had ever mentioned it to Mr. Kipling and they said that they had not, because they did not think they could get the Macmillan books.

"Here is your chance," I said, "to be generous to Mr. Kipling and give him certain rights which will not injure you. If you do this, you will keep his good will and get contributions for your magazine."

This whole Century Company row lasted for weeks, but finally we came to terms and the set was complete.

I went back to Brattleboro and presented to Mr. Kipling the different authorizations which I had secured. He was delighted, and I remember he said that I was the Cecil Rhodes of literature.

We immediately went to work and created the Outward Bound Edition, for which Mr. Kipling wrote a new preface and corrected all of his books up to date. The set was a

† George P. Brett.

great success. I would not dare to say now how many hundreds of thousands of volumes have been sold, but I am sure that Mr. Kipling must have made several hundred thousand dollars, and the Scribners certainly did not suffer.

Taking the Kipling as a cornerstone for the subscription department, in which I was so interested, I became ambitious to get the works of Robert Louis Stevenson, which in those days were not published in uniform binding. Scribner's themselves had most of the volumes, but five or six important works were owned by Roberts Brothers of Boston, and two by Stone & Kimball of Chicago. We acquired these outstanding volumes without much trouble. I think the five Roberts volumes cost us a thousand dollars apiece, and must have paid for themselves ten times over.

Another author whose works we aspired to publish in the subscription department was James Barrie, whose reputation was not very great at that time. His books had all been pirated, because the sale of several of them had not been sufficient to pay for making plates and doing the things necessary to secure copyright.

This was the start of the Scribner subscription sets, which I think really constitute the finest collection that exists in this country. If you do not believe me, take up a magazine in which the titles are enumerated and see what they include. Of course, many of them were brought into the Scribner firm after I left.

Meanwhile, the personal bickering to try to get a popular magazine against what Mr. Burlingame called a distinguished magazine went on with unabated vigor. I tried in every way I could to get more popular features and, if

I remember rightly, succeeded in only one case. I suggested that we should have a series of articles on the railroads of America, describing how they are run, and the different departments of railroad building and management. This is the only feature, I think, that we ever had which immediately took a hold on the people. It increased our circulation about twenty-five thousand, and that fell away as soon as the articles were finished, and we had nothing to take their place.

I never succeeded in getting Mr. Scribner to demand a popular magazine, which I think is not surprising, as I do not believe he knew what a popular magazine was; neither did Mr. Burlingame, nor Mr. [Robert] Bridges, his assistant, who is the editor of the magazine today. My fight for a magazine of large appeal only ended in my resignation when I left Scribner's in 1897.

I think it was in 1892 or 1893 that I went to Europe at Mr. Scribner's suggestion, particularly to arrange for the English publication of *Scribner's Magazine*. There was a time when American magazines had quite a vogue in England. The sale really was not important and gradually declined. As a matter of fact, I did not succeed in doing anything to establish *Scribner's Magazine* in London, notwithstanding that I worked very hard.

I had one experience on that trip which I shall never forget. I met Sam McClure‡ on the steamer, and he said: "There is one author in England who is not appreciated and who is a man of great distinction. You should go and get him—George Meredith."

Forthwith I went to see Mr. Meredith, and found him a

‡ S. S. McClure.

very wonderful personality. His books were highly esteemed, but the sales were small then, as I presume they
are now. I made an arrangement to publish his next book
through Scribner's, and I think it was serialized in the
magazine. The result of the visit was that Meredith became one of Scribner's authors.

One story that he told me I have never forgotten. He
said that if he could live his life over again he would write
very different books—that there was no excuse for writing
any book which did not have a substantial influence for
good. The last book that he would write, he told me, was
to be the story of a man who lived in a small country town
over which he was a sort of lord of the manor. This man
visited a friend in London who took him to Whitechapel,
and he was so much impressed with what he saw there that
he was going to give up his home and devote himself as a
missionary to work in that particular district. Naturally, he
had to conclude many arrangements at home before giving
up his residence, and in closing up his affairs he found so
much to do in the way of the welfare work of that day that
he never finished, and never got to London.

Meredith described this book with extraordinary ability,
and I eagerly hoped that it might someday be published.
But I never heard of it again, and his son told me that he
had heard nothing of it. It probably was only an idea which
Meredith never worked out.

CHAPTER III

THE SAGA
OF EDWARD THE BOK

WHEN I was about ten years old I went to Public School No. 32 in Brooklyn, and the boy who sat next to me was no less than that world figure, Edward W. Bok. His father was in the employ of the Western Union Telegraph Company as official translator, and was a man of learning and culture, quite poor, and unable to give his son the kind of education he would have wished for.

When I first knew Bok he had the seeds of amibition which blossomed later on with such prodigality. I can very well remember that he found out we had a copy of Chambers Cyclopedia, and he got us to lend him one volume at a time from which he absorbed much in the way of information. This was a significant thing, because it showed his extraordinary desire to improve himself.

Both of us left school, and I did not see nor hear of him for several years; but after I had been with Scribner's some time, Mr. Scribner introduced me to a young man whom he had employed as a stenographer, and I recognized the friend of my boyhood.

Bok was the most wonderful stenographer the world had ever seen at that time. He could take dictation as fast as anyone could talk, and wrote it out in longhand, as typewriters were unknown. It looked like copperplate, and, what is more, I believe he could spell any word ever written. His position brought him into close association with Mr. Charles Scribner, and he knew practically everything that went on. It was not more than a few months after he became a member of the staff of Scribner that his ambition began to soar; and as I was not satisfied with humdrum work myself, we commenced to put together ideas which we could work out for ourselves. I hope we were conscientious in giving Mr. Scribner his money's worth. I think my salary was sixteen dollars a week and Edward's was about fourteen.

The first thing we invented was a column of news called "Literary Leaves," made up of paragraphs more or less true about authors, and other information—or sometimes, perhaps, misinformation, but always interesting. We sold this to about fifteen or twenty newspapers, using his brother, William J. Bok, as a figurehead to sign the articles. This brought us in, I think, about thirty or forty dollars a week, which was a comfortable addition to our income.

We had many other adventures along these lines about which nobody knew, since we kept ourselves very quiet and very much in the background. Bok and I worked together for many years, putting out not only the *Book-Buyer,* but the *Presbyterian Review,* which was a big quarterly, very technical theologically. One time we sent all the *Book-Buyer* subscribers the *Presbyterian Review* by mistake, and gave the *Presbyterian Review* subscribers the *Book-Buyer*. All the people who got the *Book-Buyer* were delighted, but the people who got the *Presybterian Review* kicked.

One day a gentleman by the name of Curtis* (known as the head of the Curtis Publishing Company) appeared and wanted to see Mr. Bok. As we sat cheek by jowl, I could not help hearing the conversation. Mr. Curtis told Edward that he was the proprietor of the *Ladies' Home Journal,* which had made a great success of having the most expensive woman editor in the world—Louisa Knapp, as she was called—who was paid ten thousand dollars a year. As a matter of fact, she was Mrs. Curtis, and I do not believe she had editorial charge of the magazine; but the ten-thousand-dollar-a-year story was reprinted in hundreds of paragraphs and had its effect upon the circulation of the magazine. Now Mr. Curtis was looking for an actual editor and he had run Edward Bok to ground.

He asked Edward if he would consider an offer to become editor of the *Ladies' Home Journal* for five thousand dollars a year, with the understanding that the salary would be increased by a thousand dollars each year. Edward replied that he would be pleased to do so, since at that time, as I have said, his earnings from Scribner were about fourteen or fifteen dollars a week; but being a canny Dutchman, he demanded a contract, so that he might be sure of a job if he left Scribner's, where he had a certain income.

Mr. Curtis appeared a few days later with a contract,

* Cyrus H. K. Curtis.

and Edward asked my advice. I told him to sign it so quickly they couldn't see him for the dust. So he said he would go and get Mr. Scribner to witness it. He was gone about ten minutes, and I asked him when he came back if all had gone well. He said yes, except that he could not convince Mr. Scribner that he had been hired as an editor—he believed it was as business manager or advertising man, because nobody could possibly think that Edward Bok could be an editor. He insisted, however, upon his point, and Mr. Scribner witnessed the contract.

As he was then earning fourteen dollars a week and losing the difference between that and five thousand dollars a year, Edward asked Mr. Scribner when he could leave. But naturally Mr. Scribner had great difficulty in filling a job which had been so well covered by Bok,† and I think he kept him on a month or two, if not more, before he gave him permission to go.

As a matter of fact, the five-thousand-dollar salary was more or less of a mirage, because Curtis was nearly on the rocks at that time and Edward had trouble to collect enough to live on in Philadelphia, which should not have been much. He gradually got into the business and helped Mr. Curtis, and as everybody knows, eventually made a huge success, as well as a huge fortune.

I remember that we used to sell books to the Curtis Company which they gave away with subscriptions. They were in those days very slow pay. Our cashier, Mr. Mead, came to me one day and said he didn't wish me to sell any more books to Curtis, because he did not pay promptly; so

† At this time Bok was in charge of advertising for *Scribner's Magazine.*

I had to give up the trips that I had been making to Philadelphia to sell books.

One day the cashier said, "You can sell all the books you want to Curtis; I am sure he is solvent."

I asked him what had changed his opinion so suddenly.

He replied: "I heard that Mr. Bok was going to marry Mr. Curtis's daughter, and you can bet if they weren't solvent, Bok wouldn't marry her."

The story of Edward Bok has been written so well by himself‡ that it would be assuming too much to write any part of it again. I have known him intimately all these years, and I will take off my hat to him as the most brilliant inventor of schemes, most of them practical, all of them original, and many of them daring, that has ever been known. This was true later in life when he had large opportunities to work out schemes for the benefit of humanity, but it was equally true when he was a boy, as he admits in his own book; but I can testify that he did not exaggerate the skillfulness and cleverness of his ideas.

‡ *The Americanization of Edward Bok.*

CHAPTER IV

THE KING
OF PUBLISHERS

In the previous chapter I referred to Cyrus H. K. Curtis, who presented a contract for Bok to sign which had great results for both of them. I came to know Mr. Curtis quite intimately and had the greatest affection for him and respect for his opinion. His type of publishing is quite different from the type that I have had to do with or cared for: he was a mass publisher and is still the greatest producer of printed matter, I suppose, of any one man in the world.

He went through the hardest kind of experience. He started a paper in Boston which was entirely unsuccessful and left him plunged in debt. He then started a paper in Philadelphia, which was for a long time equally unsuccessful, and his struggles with finance would have daunted a man of less character and optimism and cheerfulness.

Perhaps next to Mr. Curtis himself, the highest praise for Mr. Curtis's success should be given to N. W. Ayer & Son. They printed advertising running into hundreds of thousands of dollars to get subscribers for his magazine, with the feeling that they would get their money back because the advertising would pay. If the advertising had not been successful, they would have lost all this money. They were always Mr. Curtis's firmest friends and are almost equally responsible for his ultimate success.

There was another man concerned with his business who played a great part in the Curtis enterprise, namely, Mr. W. H. Clarke. He trusted Mr. Curtis for hundreds of thousands of dollars' worth of paper. He, again, would have lost all his money if Mr. Curtis had not been able to pull it out. It shows, as I have often said, the necessity and value of courageous friendships.

I never saw Mr. Curtis downhearted, but I once was present when he was a little depressed and alarmed. This was brought about by the Harper debacle around 1900. It was stated at that time that Harper's had really gone into bankruptcy, which was not exactly true, but it was near enough to the truth. Curtis, although he was much more successful then, was greatly extended, and in a general collapse of the publishing trade nobody knows what might have happened to him. I was with him the day the announcement was made, as I was anxious to be out of New York when the reporters began to ask questions about Harper's. I think Mr. Curtis was really worried that day, but the excitement passed over in forty-eight hours and caused him no inconvenience so far as I ever heard.

One extraordinary characteristic Mr. Curtis always had: that is, he would select a man for a job, put him in control, and back him without reserve. Of course, as long as you strike the right man, this is not a very risky business; but if you make a mistake, it is fatal. Curtis may have made some mistakes, but not enough to injure the business, which I presume is much the largest of any publishing concern. He is now seventy-five years old; as chipper as a lark; dashing in to correct one department after another; going off on long trips on his yacht without any direct communication with the business, telegraph or otherwise; and in general managing his affairs with superb courage and success.

He told me the story of his purchase of the New York *Evening Post,* which was characteristic. He wanted to secure the services of one of the editors of the *Post,* so he went to Tom Lamont, of J. P. Morgan & Company, who owned the paper, and told him that he did not wish to do anything unfriendly, but he did wish to hire this particular individual.

Tom Lamont said, "Why don't you buy the whole paper? Then you can have this man and everything that goes with him."

"All right," said Curtis, and they came to an agreement forthwith.

Whether he has made any money on the New York *Evening Post,* I doubt, but I would be willing to bet a red apple that if he devoted himself to the paper, he would make a success of it.

Of course, after he achieved a real circulation for the *Saturday Evening Post* and the *Ladies' Home Journal* and the *Country Gentleman* he wanted something else to amuse him, as running these periodicals seemed to him a little stale. So he bought the Philadelphia *Ledger,* which he told me helped his income tax for a long time. Now he has built huge structures for his publications in Philadelphia and a big one in New York for the *Evening Post.*

He is a delightful and sweet character. One of his favorite amusements is improvising on the organ, and he plays, I should say, mighty well in his own peculiar style. May he live long and prosper.

CHAPTER V

THE BREAK
WITH SCRIBNER

As TIME went on I became more and more unhappy in my relations with Mr. Scribner. Finally Nellie* said, "I would prefer to scrub floors than see you go on with Scribner's the way you are now doing. I am absolutely positive that you could be as successful for yourself as you are now with Scribner's."

It required a tremendous amount of courage to give up a definite salary; I think I was making about eight or ten thousand dollars a year, and a commission of eight per cent on the profits of my two departments, *Scribner's Magazine* and the subscription book department, which at that time was quite a little fortune: at all events, it had to support a lot of people.†

Having finally got my nerve up to the sticking point, I told Mr. Scribner that I proposed to leave to go into business for myself. He was surprised and shocked and

* Neltje De Graff Doubleday, his first wife.
† F.N.D. had numerous dependents at that point.

grieved; I don't think anything of the sort had ever occurred to him. He said that he had given me his confidence, and it was disloyal of me to take the experience that I had acquired with him and use it for my own benefit in my own business.

I replied that perhaps I had a moral laxity, but that I was going to do it.

He asked me what my plans were.

I told him that I had no plans; I considered it my first duty to come and tell him that I was going to leave. He became very angry and said that I had better leave that afternoon. I told him that I had been there eighteen years, and I was not willing to leave until I had said good-by to my friends and put my papers and affairs in shape to turn over to my successor.

The next morning, much to my surprise, he offered me a partnership. As the Scribner family had never had a real partner, this was a tremendous affair, and was considered by Mr. Scribner as being the greatest compliment that he had ever paid to anyone.

I told him that I would consider it and talk it over with my wife, which I did. We decided that, having started on our own, we would keep it up.

The next day, having already left his employ, I presented myself to Mr. Scribner to tell him what I had decided; but before I could speak he said: "I offered you a partnership yesterday, but I have changed my mind. I don't think it would work, and I hereby withdraw it."

I said this was entirely satisfactory to me, as I had decided to decline to enter into partnership with him.

He was furious, and almost put me out of his office. That was the last time I saw him for some months.

I had had many discussions with Mr. Robert M. Fair, Mrs. Doubleday's uncle, and a wise old fellow, whose advice was of inestimable value to me; and he promised, if I decided to leave Scribner's and start in business for myself, to lend me five thousand dollars.

I also asked the advice of Mr. A. L. Hollingsworth, a paper manufacturer and a very old friend of mine, about going into business for myself. He said he thought it was a foolish idea—that I was making too much money to risk giving up my job. "But," he said, "if you do go into business, I will lend you two thousand dollars and give you credit for all the paper you need."

Naturally, I was deeply appreciative, and—later—horror-stricken when I found that he had been to see Mr. Scribner and told him what he had offered to do for me, as he said he wished to be aboveboard in all his dealings.

Mr. Scribner's reply was that he would never buy another pound of paper from the Tileston & Hollingsworth Company, and he never did; but I am thankful to say that Doubleday & McClure Company and Doubleday, Page & Company bought hundreds of thousands of dollars' worth of paper, so in the end my friend did not lose.

Another friend in the paper business was Mr. William F. Etherington. He was also a friend of Mr. F. Coit Johnson. Mr. Johnson invited us to the Wool Club one day to discuss the question as to whether, without much capital and with plenty of expenses and responsibilities in the way of a large family, it was wise for me to start out for myself. Mr. Etherington felt, as Mr. Hollingsworth did, that the risks were great; but he, also, offered to give me all the credit I needed for the purchase of paper. I am thankful that he did not tell Mr. Scribner, and I am thankful, also, that we have bought from him millions of dollars' worth of paper for our books and magazines.

CHAPTER VI

OUTSIDE INTERESTS

IF THIS BOOK should have any readers, they might easily get the impression that I had no interest in the world beyond the publishing business, as every page appears to be devoted to this enticing subject. As a matter of fact, it is quite true that the publishing business absorbed most of my time and thought—it had to. I had many responsibilities of a monetary sort which had to be provided for, and the publishing trade was the only way I knew to make a living.

But I did have other interests. I was a great player of tennis and golf, and a pretty regular performer in the New York Bay as a swimmer. I was also a traveler whenever opportunity presented itself. In those days anybody who had to do with a periodical could, if he was cheeky enough, get free transportation. Those really were the days of the passover; I had many passes both for myself and my family, and worked them diligently. My only regret was that I never could get a pass from the Pullman Palace Car Company; I had to pay them real cash—a tragic proceeding.

Another thing that always interested me very much was

local town affairs. I remember that after we moved to Long Island I had a particular desire to help in any way I could to bring the city residents who had large estates into association with the local people—a pretty difficult job. One time we attempted to give a little party for both classes, and on that occasion only the local people came.

One of the latter urged me strongly to help him to establish a church. There was at the time a Dutch Reformed church which had been closed for several years and was only opened for special occasions. I had no experience in helping churches, and I am afraid tennis and golf kept me away from the services more than they should have; but I realized that a town like Locust Valley should have a church, and I offered to help them if they would combine with the church some welfare work which would be practical and which was much needed in the village.

My first job was to find a pastor who would preach, visit his parishioners, and conduct the affairs of the Neighborhood Association all at the same time for one salary. I remember I did not think much about denominations, but I went to the Presbyterian Building in New York to inquire where they kept their unattached clergymen suitable for a country job. The only person that they had in stock who seemed to fill that bill was the Reverend E. Fred Eastman, who was born and brought up in the Middle West and was not too hidebound for my purposes. I was very favorably impressed with him when I met him and very anxious to get him to take the job, but I began by making a bad mistake. I took him in a car all around Locust Valley, showing him the biggest places, and expatiating on the wealth of their owners, with the idea of making him feel that we had substantial backing for our enterprise in the way of contributions.

He seemed not very much impressed, and finally said: "So far as I can see, if I take this job, I shall become a theological lap dog controlled by the rich people of the community."

Therefore, I had to begin all over again, and I took him to see the natives, and explained that these were the people who were going to be helped.

In addition to this, I gave a dinner at the Piping Rock Club, sandwiching in the estate owners and the old natives of the town. This was the most curious dinner that has ever been held at the Piping Rock. A blacksmith sat next to Mr. Coffin, the president of the General Electric Company; a candy and soda man sat next to Mr. Hodenpyl, our very prosperous friend and a real gentleman, etc., etc. But we had a great time and everybody was quite at ease, and I think this was the reason Eastman finally accepted and undertook the job. The waiters could not understand such a mixed company and were all terribly embarrassed.

He conducted the affairs of the church and the affairs of the welfare association with skill and success for a number of years; but it eventually turned out that these things could not be combined in the way that I had hoped. This is no particular matter, for the church is today much more successful, and the Matinecock Neighborhood Association goes on with its work with equal success. There was one rather interesting thing in connection with the building of Matinecock House. Many people in Locust Valley were anxious to contribute liberally, but could not afford the ready money, so we accepted contributions of one or two

weeks' work from carpenters, plumbers, and other trades-
men. Altogether, I think the building cost about thirty
thousand dollars and has been a success from the first—
more so today, probably, than at any other time.

CHAPTER VII

STARTING BUSINESS
FOR MYSELF

DOUBLEDAY & McCLURE COMPANY

It happened in March 1897, and I shall never forget it. I cut myself loose from Scribner's and a salary. I put up a brave front, but to tell the truth, I was deeply alarmed at my position. I have sympathy for people who lose their jobs or give them up when they have for years counted on a stated salary. I think even the strongest are apt to be put in a funk through this experience. However, I began to stir around to see what I could do, and I talked with S. S. McClure, who told me that he had heard I had left Scribner's. I said that I had, and I was going to establish my own business.

He invited me to come with him on his magazine, and offered me a salary of five thousand dollars a year. This put me at ease at once, and I moved from Fifth Avenue to the Power House on Lexington Avenue, taking my hat and coat, the only goods I had. I did not know where Mr. McClure was to get the five thousand, as his business was in a precarious position; but I hoped that I would be able to help him, and I think in a small way I did.

I was given three per cent of the stock of *McClure's Magazine* besides my five-thousand-dollar salary, and in return I gave Mr. McClure forty-nine per cent of the stock of the new Doubleday & McClure Company, who were to be publishers of books.

So I started in at once to help as I could on the magazine, and to create a list of publications. I had several important assets. In the first place, I knew something about the business, having had a long experience. In the second place, Mr. Fair had promised to loan me five thousand dollars, Mr. Hollingsworth two thousand, Mr. Etherington five thousand and a lot of credit for all the paper I really needed.

Following out the principle in which I have always believed, of employing the best instead of the cheapest, I made an arrangement with T. L. De Vinne & Company, who were regarded as the most distinguished and perhaps the most expensive printers in New York, to make our books. They did good work, and I think helped us considerably in our start.

With the same idea of trying, whenever I made a connection, to associate myself with the best, I inquired which was the finest bank in New York, and was told the Chemical. As usual, I got a letter of introduction and went to the bank.

I saw Mr. Williams, the president, a one-eyed and very kindly old gentleman, who appeared to be interested in my story and very friendly. He asked what he could do for me. I said:

"Can you loan me five thousand dollars, which I will repay in six months?"

"Have you any collateral?" he inquired.

"Nothing but my reputation," I replied, "which is fairly good, and my experience, which goes over eighteen years."

Whereupon he said, "Well, I am going to help you."

"I am greatly obliged to you, Mr. Williams," I said, "and, more than that, I am going to be a stockholder in your bank."

As it turned out, we have been stockholders for many years, having paid, I think, about four thousand dollars a share.

Here, then, was the position in March 1897. Including my paper-making friends, the bank, and Uncle Robert, I had a possible capital of something between twenty and thirty thousand dollars, and a temporary salary to help along week by week.

S. S. MCCLURE

I would like to stop here and describe my friend and partner, Samuel S. McClure, who with John S. Phillips and Albert B. Brady composed the concern of S. S. Mc-Clure Company. I had known Sam McClure for many years and had had many experiences with him. He was a very extraordinary man, with a wonderful eye for a new author and the keenest appreciation of literature. He had many fruitful, excellent, and courageous ideas, but he lacked the quality to bind them together to make a success.

McClure's Magazine was an example of his original type of mind. Up to that time nobody had ever thought of printing anything in a magazine which was not written for it. Sam McClure believed that if the stuff was good—even if it had been printed weeks or years before in the newspapers—and if collected in attractive form, it would find a good as well as an extensive market. When I say a good market, I mean people who would appreciate good literature. In this way he published many of the best authors, like Robert Louis Stevenson, Rudyard Kipling, and men of the highest type, although he had just printed the same material in a newspaper syndicate.

This was only one example of his originality and courage. He was erratic to the last degree, and to be his partner was something like sitting on the top of a volcano with a very hot interior. But I had pleasant relations with him for three years, notwithstanding that we had the most violent disagreements, and I insisted upon keeping the control of Doubleday & McClure Company. It was lucky for me that I did, or it would have been squandered as the S. S. McClure Company was dissipated until nothing remained of it.

In addition to his great ability and feeling for good literature, Sam had a very warm heart. He was always helping somebody out, although he had so very little money to spend. Dozens of times I have known him to buy written material because a man needed the money, when as a matter of fact he needed the money himself just as badly.

There are hundreds of stories told about him, most of which I think were true. This one, at least, is, because I was associated with the whole of the transaction. Sam got the idea that a new life of Christ would be very successful.

After a great deal of trouble he induced Elizabeth Stuart Phelps* to agree to undertake the job. She sent in the first half dozen chapters, which disappointed Sam extremely. He wrote to her that she would never be able to write a life of Christ, as she could not possibly "make it snappy enough." What he really meant was that it should have the character and popularity of a book like Papini's,† published successfully twenty-five years later.

I remember one experience when even S.S. was floored completely. We were anxious to get some more bank loans, and my friend, F. Coit Johnson, suggested that we should go to a certain bank in which he had a large account. He went to the president and told him that he knew of a young firm which had just started, which was going to be a great institution and would be a valuable depositor; and he would give him the name and address so that he could solicit the account.

Greatly to our surprise, a gentleman from this bank called on us and asked us to come down and see the president. This, I think, was within a week or two of our having been refused a loan of twenty-five hundred dollars from the Astor Place Bank, and our financial condition was very depressed.

I got hold of John Phillips and Sam McClure, and we went down to see what the manager of the Central National Bank wanted. Sam was frightened, and John was astonished; but I had been given a cue and was not in a complete state of collapse.

* Author of a best seller, *The Gates Ajar*.
† Giovanni Papini, *Life of Christ* (1923).

The president said that he would like to show us the bank and tell us something about it, which was the first surprise we had. He took us through the building and explained the operation of the different departments, and finally said that he would like us to open an account.

Sam almost fainted. He kept absolutely mum. It ended by our opening an account with five thousand dollars of the bank's money, and we did business with them for many years, I hope to their advantage. I never saw Sam so flabbergasted. He was afraid to speak for fear something would happen that would take that five thousand dollars away from him.

One thing that Sam insisted upon was that I should go to Europe and get some authors both for the magazine and for our book list. The one author that we really needed to put us on the map was Rudyard Kipling. As related, I had had some experience with him on the Outward Bound Edition, but this was a very different affair.

So we took ship, and immediately went to see Kipling, who was at St. Mary Church in the southern part of England. I urged that he should give us his new book, which afterwards turned out to be *The Day's Work*. My arguments were injured by the fact that he had four publishers already. He knew that I was able to sell books, and I think was prejudiced in my favor, particularly when I told him that if he gave us this book we would *have* to sell it, otherwise our business would not be a success.

He finally turned me over to A. P. Watt, his literary agent, who, greatly to my surprise, recommended that Mr. Kipling should make a contract with me to publish *The*

Day's Work, with an advance of five hundred pounds. I did not know where I was to get the five hundred pounds, but I eagerly accepted and closed the contract forthwith.

This was a tremendous help to us. We published it in the fall of 1898, and it was an immediate success and sold at once over a hundred thousand copies, far exceeding anything his books had reached up to that time. We have published every one of his books from that day to this.

While we were on that trip we picked up a number of good books and new connections—nothing that I remember of very special importance, but we started associations which turned out later to be valuable.

RUNNING HARPER & BROTHERS

One of the most important episodes that I had with Sam McClure was really amusing as well as tragic. One day I was in a telephone booth getting a long-distance call to Philadelphia, when he attracted my attention by knocking on the glass and insisting upon it that I should quit the telephone and come into his office. As I had a seventy-five-cent call in, I hated to lose the money; but he made such a fuss about it that eventually I did.

There I found a red-haired, good-natured, fat individual whom McClure introduced as Mr. Sleeper Harper, treasurer of Harper. I thought that he lived up to his name.

Sam said, "Frank, Mr. Sleeper Harper wants us to take over the business of Harper & Brothers."

I could easily have been floored with the traditional feather. I turned to Mr. Harper, surprised into an expression which I should not have given vent to, and said, "Mr.

Harper, are you in as bad a condition as that?" What occurred to me was that, if anybody wanted us to take over a business, it must be on its last legs.

Mr. Harper said that it was not that his business was in such a bad state but that they had borrowed from Mr. Morgan some eight or nine hundred thousand dollars; he was not satisfied with the way the business was being conducted, and suggested that the McClure business and Harper & Brothers should be put together. It did not take me very long to realize that if anybody wanted to combine a business with ours it must be a pretty poor affair, and my examination of the books proved this to be true.

I stubbornly refused to have anything to do with it. What I believe to have been Mr. Morgan's idea was that if we put our little business in with Harper we would have to pull the whole thing out or lose what we had.

Sam was eager to get a sensational reputation by buying out Harper, and we finally made a compact. We were to run the concern on a salary of thirty-six thousand dollars a year, and in turn were to pay thirty-six thousand dollars a year for an option to purchase the business at a price which I have now forgotten, but I presume it was about five times what it was worth.

The papers made a fuss about it the next day, and we found ourselves with the job of running this old and moribund concern. I think the first six months we cut down expenses something more than a hundred thousand dollars, not withstanding which the business lost at least an equal sum. The further we went into the study of the figures, the worse they became. I think they had notes outstanding in every country bank in the United States, amounting to almost a million and a half dollars. They were even back on their taxes, not being able to pay the city tax bill. I was for getting out, and telegraphed Sam, who was in Europe (he had left home as soon as he signed the contract with Harper) that the job was impossible— to come back at once. He replied that he loved to do the impossible and would return forthwith. But even he was convinced, when we showed him the figures, that the business could not be pulled out without something like fifteen or twenty years' work.

We therefore went to Mr. Morgan's lawyer, collected our salary as far as it had been earned, turned it over in payment for the option which we did not want, and went back to our own jobs.

I have been much interested in this property ever since, and have had several experiences in connection with it. I think that perhaps we made a mistake: if we had raised sufficient capital, which we could have done through Mr. Morgan's influence, we might have made a success of it. But undoubtedly it would have been a stiff job, and with Sam's erratic ways it would have been very difficult to hold the control in such a way that it could be successfully managed.

One thing that it showed me, which was revealed again in our purchase of the McClure Company, was the value of a good list. You can do almost anything with a book publishing house if it has a substantial list, provided you are clever enough to manage it properly.

Several times in later years the Harper business was brought to our attention, but nothing ever came of it, and considering the chances for nervous prostration that it afforded, I think perhaps it was just as well.

PRESIDENT MCKINLEY'S SPEECHES

Early in the history of Doubleday & McClure Company I had an experience which I do not understand even to this day. I received a message from Mr. Porter, President McKinley's private secretary, that the President wished to see me in Washington at nine o'clock the next day. I immediately telephoned that the message must have been meant for somebody else; that I did not know the President, I was not looking for a job, and there must be some mistake.

I then had a second telephone call from Mr. Porter that the President wanted to see me especially about the publication of a book; so I took the midnight train to Washington and was at the White House at nine o'clock.

Mr. Porter shut the door and closed the transom, and made everything very secret; and told me that the President wanted to have a book published and had selected us as his publishers.

This made me deeply suspicious, as we had been in business only a few months and I could not imagine why he should come to such insignificant people as ourselves. I attempted to develop the subject, but it was all sheathed in mystery and I could not get out of the White House what the book was about.

I made several trips at the President's request before I found out that what he wanted was to have a book of his speeches published and paid for by the National Republican Campaign Committee. When I got as far as this I went to Senator Hanna‡ and said: "What does all this mean, and where do I get off or get on?"

He then described the President's plan, and said that he did not like to mention the fact that the Campaign Committee was to pay the bill. He asked me if the book would sell, and I told him it would not. He said he thought that I was right.

Eventually we made a contract to print the speeches in an elaborate and beautiful book, manufactured by De Vinne, and the edition, I think, was about two thousand copies. When it was all finished, I asked Senator Hanna what I should do with it, and he said, "Pack up the books, put on the enclosed express frank, and send them to me," which I did. I have never heard of a copy of that book from that day to this. I think he threw them into Lake Erie and that was the end of the episode. Who had given the President our name, or why he had us do the job, is beyond me. I presume the book is rare and scarce now.

The Doubleday & McClure Company was really quite successful, considering the smallness of affairs in those days. It lasted for three years, from 1897 to 1900, when Doubleday, Page & Company was established. I think the last year we made a profit of about forty thousand dollars, and going was good.

Perhaps the final item of interest with Doubleday & McClure Company was the sale to Claflin of fifteen thousand sets of twelve volumes of Kipling. As will be related in another place, Mr. Kipling was ill at the Grenoble Hotel in 1899, and I suggested to him one day that we should get up another set of his works to supply the readers who

‡ Senator Mark Hanna of Ohio, chairman of the committee.

wanted a cheaper collection than the Outward Bound. He agreed that the idea was a good one, but he did not see how we could do the contents of the Outward Bound Edition over again in a low-priced set. I confess that it was difficult, but I secured an order from the H. B. Claflin Company, who had just gone into the book business, for fifteen thousand sets at six dollars a set. By another exhibition of enormous cheek, I got permission from the Century Company, Appleton, and Macmillan to print this set by giving them a percentage of the profit.

Very much to my chagrin, the set did not sell well, and a year or two afterwards Claflin came to me and offered to sell us the remainder, which I think amounted to four or five thousand sets, for three dollars a set.

My faith in Kipling's popularity was unbounded, and I was glad to accept their offer and put the stock away. The moment I withdrew the set from the market it seemed to take on new value; but we declined to supply any copies, I think, for six months or so. During this time the orders accumulated, and when we felt that the opportunity was ripe, we put it back on the market and sold the whole stock for a very good price and cleared up quite a lot of money.

CHAPTER VIII

THE FRIENDSHIP
OF ANDREW CARNEGIE

As I LOOK BACK on my long life, I can remember few people who did me such a great service as Andrew Carnegie. His ideas were clever as well as foundationally sound, and during my long friendship with him I was tremendously benefited.

My first meeeting came through his connection with Scribner's. He had written one book called *Triumphant Democracy*—an original affair, the kind of thing that Henry Ford writes now—and it was quite successful. I had the job of doing the advertising, and Mr. Carnegie turned over to me a large sum of money to spend in making the book known.

I was deeply interested in it and his other writings and suggested that he should undertake another book called *The Empire of Business,* using his articles which had appeared in the newspapers, speeches, etc., on the subject of business in its various aspects. He assented to the idea, and I arranged for the contents and I think Russell

Doubleday edited the book, which was quite as successful as his *Triumphant Democracy*. Thus began a long friendship which included many games of golf, for, like most Scotsmen, he was very fond of the game, and I was always interested in playing with him.

When I began to think of leaving Scribner's, I wrote to Mr. Carnegie and asked him if he thought that without education or capital I could make a success. He was positive in his advice, and urged me strongly and emphatically to give up my job with Scribner's and start my own publishing house. He believed, he said, that I was the type of man who would do well as my own boss and as the creator of an organization, which was the important part. When I actually came to leave Scribner's his words gave me great courage, and I really feel that I owe him undying thanks for giving me this lift.

I remember that I asked him about this time how to work a bank for a loan. He said, "Pick out the best bank in New York, walk in on your heels, and make them understand that you are doing them a favor by borrowing money from them."

I said this sounded easy, but they might not be so enthusiastic as he thought.

He replied that if they did not lend me the money I could say that Andrew Carnegie would.

I protested that I had not brought up the subject with that idea in mind.

He stopped me and said, "My son, let me give you a piece of advice. When you see things coming your way, never interfere." And to the best of my ability, all these years I have lived up to his advice.

I had many extraordinary experiences with him. Perhaps the most extraordinary was a connection with the sale of the Carnegie Steel Company to the United States Steel Trust. My relation with the matter I did not know of until weeks afterwards.

One day I received a message from Mr. Carnegie that he would like me to play golf with him the next morning, and to meet him at his house at precisely ten o'clock. It was a cold winter's day, and I was not particularly anxious to play at St. Andrews, where we were accustomed to go, but I was at his house promptly.

His secretary came down to see me and said that he thought Mr. Carnegie would not be able to play that day, because he had some important business with Mr. J. P. Morgan, who was now with Mr. Carnegie in his library.

I said I would go then, as I was not eager to play myself.

"Wait a minute," he said; "I will tell Mr. Carnegie."

He came back shortly and said: "Mr. Carnegie wants you to wait. He will leave the house with you at the usual time and catch the usual train."

Presently Mr. Carnegie appeared; we went by electric automobile to the station, and made the journey to St. Andrews where we played nine holes. Afterwards we had luncheon, and he followed his invariable custom of taking a nap, while I was permitted to smoke a cigar, of which he cordially disapproved.

He said nothing to me of his affairs, or of his interview with Mr. Morgan, but several weeks later his secretary asked me if I would be interested to know what happened that day that we went to St. Andrews at ten o'clock in the morning.

I said that I would.

It appears that when he went back to tell Mr. Carnegie that I was downstairs, Mr. Carnegie turned to Mr. Morgan and said, "Mr. Morgan, I have told you the terms on which I would sell the Carnegie Steel Company. If you are favorable to the idea, we will close the deal. If not, I will ask you to excuse me, as I have made an engagement and my friend is waiting for me downstairs."

Morgan was rather flabbergasted at this blunt statement and said he would accept Mr. Carnegie's offer.

The Scotsman thereupon dictated the agreement to his secretary, Mr. Bertram, who wrote it down in shorthand. He asked Mr. Bertram how much space it would take on a sheet of foolscap, and Mr. Bertram said it would all easily go on one page. Whereupon Mr. Carnegie said, "Give me two sheets of foolscap, and I will sign both of them. Then you can type the agreement over my signature, and get Mr. Morgan to sign it, keep one copy, and give the other to the banker."

Bertram was highly pleased to be entrusted with such an important piece of business requiring both cleverness and integrity (I think it involved about three hundred million dollars), and was eager to tell me the story; otherwise I should never have heard it from that day to this, as in all my intercourse with Mr. Carnegie it was a story he never told me. Of course, involving as it did such a huge sum of money, within a few days the newspapers were full of it.

About this time we had invited Mr. and Mrs. Carnegie

and Mr. and Mrs. Clemens (Mark Twain) to dinner at our house on East Sixteenth Street. It was a rather embarrassing dinner as it turned out. Knowing little of the tastes of plutocrats in the way of spirituous liquors, I had provided champagne, and Mr. Carnegie asked for some whisky, which I did not happen to have in the house. The children were in the pantry waiting for ice cream, and I told one of them to dash out and get a bottle of the best whisky he could at the Westminster Hotel. He returned with a bottle, which was served by the waitress in a sherry glass, and it required a good deal of attention to get it in the proper receptacle. The result was finally presented to Mr. Carnegie, who smelled it, turned up his nose, and said: "You know I can't drink rye whisky."

His wife turned to him and said: "You drink that whisky, Andrew, and make no more fuss about it"—which he did.

Meanwhile, Mark Twain was very amusing. He told Mr. Carnegie that he had read in a newspaper that he was prosperous; that he (Mark) needed a new prayer book, and he wanted Mr. Carnegie to give him the price, which he said would be a dollar and a half.

Mr. Carnegie said, "I will do better than that; I will give you a handsome prayer book selected by myself."

"No," Mark said, "I want the dollar and a half that it costs."

So finally Mr. Carnegie agreed to give it to him.

One day when we were playing golf at St. Andrews, Mr. Carnegie turned to me and asked in his modest Scotch way: "How much money did you make in your book business last month?"

I told him I could not tell—that no publisher made up his books more than once a year, and it was impossible to figure the profits month by month.

He said: "Do you know what I would do if I were in a business in which I couldn't tell the amount of monthly profit?"

"No," I replied; "what would you do?"

"I would get out of it," he said.

This had a great effect on me and a great effect on our business. We immediately set to work to organize our accounting department so that we could tell our condition at the end of each month. It may seem easy now, but it was a gigantic task then, full of difficulties and unexpected troubles. It took us a year or two before we finally got the system working correctly.

In 1899, as all the world knows, Mr. Kipling was very ill of double pneumonia at the Grenoble Hotel in New York. I had promised Mrs. Kipling that I would stay with him until he was well, and do the best I could in the errand-boy kind of service that is needed in a sickroom.

The first job I had was to find the best whisky obtainable in New York. I was quite convinced that Mr. Carnegie would have this, so I went to see him. He expressed himself as delighted to furnish the liquor, and he did furnish it all through Mr. Kipling's long and severe illness.

One day after Kipling got to the stage where he lay on the sofa, I said to him: "Shouldn't we have in Mr. Carnegie and thank him for all this whisky of his that you have had?"

He agreed that it was a good idea, so I went to Mr. Carnegie and invited him to call. He asked me just what kind of man Mr. Kipling was, and I told him that he was very shy, and he would only get along well if he talked about other subjects than Mr. Kipling's own books or himself.

When he arrived he stood in the middle of the room— Mr. Kipling being on the sofa, with my hand attached to his pulse—and very pompously orated as follows:

"Mr. Kipling, I regard this as one of the greatest honors that has come to me in my life. That I should have been able to serve you in this small way has been the greatest pleasure to me, and as Shakespeare put it in his immortal verse—as Shakespeare put it in his immortal verse—"

He could not remember what Shakespeare put in his immortal verse, and Mr. Kipling's pulse was mounting by leaps and bounds.

"—or as Burns expresses it in his well-known poem— as Burns expresses it in his well-known—"

He could not remember what Burns expressed, and I thought Rudyard's life would go out.

I broke up the speech by inquiring, "Mr. Carnegie, how is the steel business?"

He at once settled down and the strain was over, and Mr. Kipling's pulse returned to somewhere near normal; but I certainly was very frightened.

When he left he said to both of us, "You must come and visit us at Skibo Castle."

I said, "Why, Mr. Carnegie, have you got two spare rooms?"

He threw up his hands and replied, "Why, it is a *castle,* man, with scores of rooms."

At the end of the last century Nellie and I made a burst into New York society. The papers did not record the fact, and unless I tell it here the story might be submerged and never be heard of. I want my children to know that their father and mother did crash New York society and came out alive on the other side.

We were invited to the Carnegies' to dinner, so we hired a "coach" with two horses and a fellow with a high hat—the whole thing was the sort of business that they used at funerals. We had been told that swell people in New York society never arrived on time for dinner. We nearly broke this rule by getting there too quickly, but we drove around until the time arrived and five minutes had passed besides.

I found that I was elected to take in to the dining table a lady whose name was Kennedy. I think she was the wife of a great banker in Wall Street. I had dimly heard of her but had not heard very much. She was certainly impressive and her avoirdupois was abundant. We no sooner sat down than she began to ask me questions, and as I was anxious to appear well in New York society, I was careful with my replies. She asked me where I lived and I told her on East Sixteenth Street. She inquired if that was a nice neighborhood, and I said, "Fairly good, but not too good." Somehow she got the impression that I was a settlement worker living on the East Side, and as she had taken that cue, I filled the part as well as I could. I was under constant embarrassment, as she sat on my right side and was particularly billowy—I was immensely curious but did not like to look too close. On the other side was a lady who talked scandal and scared me to death by her frankness; and so this young man from the East Side, the settlement worker in the palace of the rich, had a rather trying time to keep his head and eyes where they belonged.

After a while I began to ask Mrs. Kennedy questions. I told her that this was my first burst into society, and any advice that she could give me I should be grateful to receive. She then informed me how dinner parties were given in the swellest places in England, and how after dinner the ladies withdrew and the gentlemen had their coffee alone. I thanked her very much for giving me this information, because I might otherwise have gone out with the ladies, which would have embarrassed her.

She then told me about her place at Bar Harbor, which she said was very beautiful, and that she had an Italian garden. I told her that we had an Italian garden in our little country place. "Are you sure it is an Italian garden?" she asked. I said, "Yes, I am absolutely sure; it took two Italians two days to make it."

So we went on gossiping. At the end of the dinner Andrew Carnegie's bagpipe player came in with a huge noise and marched around the table. This was the form that most of the people there had accustomed themselves to, but I think it was a surprise to Mrs. Kennedy. Then we were all instructed to leave the room together and go into the drawing room. I declined to go with Mrs. Kennedy because I said I was not going to make a mistake after being told that the ladies went out and left the gentlemen. The poor old hen was in a lot of trouble, but I stuck it out, and with one other man stayed behind to smoke.

Carnegie hated smoking worse than poison, and we had had only five minutes with our cigars when he blustered in and made us come into the drawing room and behave ourselves.

We got home safely. Thus did the Doubleday family make their first move in the swell circles of New York. They have since had an opportunity to dine with the great, but I think never have I had so embarrassing an experience at a dinner party.

CHAPTER IX

MY LIFELONG INTIMACY
WITH RUDYARD KIPLING

To WRITE what I should like to write about Rudyard Kipling, my pen would have to be shod with fire. There are one or two fortunate things, however, which will help out. As this book is written for my family, and they all know Mr. Kipling and have had innumerable experiences with him (or with "Uncle Rud" as the children call him), they do not have to depend on anything that I may write here to add to their affection and love for him.

Another source of knowledge is the Kipling material in the green safe. Here is the manuscript of *The Light That Failed;* rare editions that he himself has given me; one of only two sets (the other one made for Mr. Kipling himself) of the complete Outward Bound Edition on special paper and dedicated to me by Mr. Kipling; and a mass of correspondence that tells the whole tale; so if this chapter is not especially revealing, there still remains material to complete the story.

My relations with Kipling were twofold. In the first

place, I was his publisher and had more or less business with him, though the actual arrangements for the publication of his books were carried out through his agent, Mr. A. P. Watt, and afterwards with Mr. Aleck Watt. But in addition to this, I knew him intimately as a friend, although it is quite true that during all the thirty years of our friendship we have seen each other comparatively little except on one particular occasion.

As I have already said, I met Mr. Kipling in arranging the publication and collection of the Outward Bound Edition. We had had some correspondence and had tried hard to make a unique and attractive book, which I think we succeeded in doing; at all events, its success indicates that much.

When the Doubleday & McClure Company was started, the help that Mr. Kipling could give us was obvious; but it seemed unlikely that such a great author with four publishers would leave them for another and young publisher whose fortune and success were still to be achieved—and we were particularly lacking in cash. But I had gaily sailed over to England, with the fond hope that I would come back with his new book in my pocket, and, as described, went to St. Mary Church and without serious difficulty procured a contract. Of course, he gave us the greatest kind of a start, as a Kipling book then, as now, was a literary event.

In the winter of 1898–1899, Mr. Kipling came to visit America. His wife was born and brought up in Vermont, and as an American she thought that it was their duty to bring their children to this country to see their old American friends. This turned out to be a serious affair, because everyone invited him to dinner, tea, and every sort of entertainment. I remember that even we were guilty, and gave him a large dinner where we played him up as the chief lion of the occasion.

This went on for a couple of weeks, during which he went out every night, entertained to the point of desperation.

About Washington's Birthday, 1899, he came down with pneumonia. Although I knew him well, I thought I was not in a position to do much to help him, and I shall never forget the evening of Washington's Birthday, when I went to the Grenoble Hotel in New York where they were staying (one of the worst hotels, by the way, in existence at that time) and found Mrs. Kipling in desperate shape. Her husband had developed double pneumonia; her oldest child, Josephine, also had pneumonia; John had a cold which they suspected was pneumonia; and Elsie, the youngest of all, was not well.

To find themselves in a New York hotel in this position was about as tragic and sad as anything could be. I told Mrs. Kipling that I would do anything I could to help. She asked me how long I could stay, and I told her that I would stay until Rud was well.

We immediately set to work organizing medical arrangements. A friend, Miss De Forest, took Josephine, and the other children were made as comfortable as possible. We succeeded in getting Dr. Janeway, who was the most eminent physician of his day, and an assistant physician, Theodore Dunham, who was a member of the Balestier family, and two or three trained nurses. Mrs. Kipling was one of the greatest organizers I have ever met. Within a day the whole enterprise of looking after these various sick people was in smooth working order, with the very best skills that New York could provide.

My job was to take care of the nurses; see that people were fed; provide plenty of whisky of the finest quality from Mr. Carnegie's cellar; and do whatever was necessary to keep the ball going. One of the most difficult tasks of all was to see the reporters twice a day. The illness made a great sensation and columns were printed about it on the first pages of the newspapers. I recall that I was so tired that I could not remember my own name. I slept on the floor just outside of the sickroom, and was busy with these various enterprises until I almost passed away.

The whole thing is a horror in my mind, and I rather hate to think of it; but in the end Mr. Kipling's life was saved, although Josephine died.

It is not difficult to imagine the intimacy which came about through this constant association, which lasted three months. I do not think I went to my office for at least two months, and I finally delivered him to his home in Rottingdean, near Brighton, England.

Notwithstanding all the terrible things that happened in traveling through the Valley of the Shadow of Death, there were some amusing things, too. I remember I came into the room after Kipling was quite convalescent, and the nurse put her finger to her lips so that I should not disturb the patient. As he was progressing very favorably and was well on his way toward recovery, I was surprised at this. She handed me the clinical thermometer and I looked at it with horror. It was 107°. I almost fainted, when a voice from the bed said, "The result of putting your thermometer in the breakfast tea." It frightened the nurse as much as it frightened me.

One special privilege I had that was particularly pleasing to me. The doctors came every morning and thumped Mr. Kipling's chest to see if the inflammation was receding. One day he said to them, "Now you can thump my chest all you wish, but I want something in return."

"What do you want?" asked Dr. Janeway.

He replied, "I want to be left alone an hour a day with my friend Frank, when we can have a little private tête-à-tête of our own."

This the doctor agreed to, and every morning about eleven o'clock I lifted Mr. Kipling out of bed, took him in the next room, and we settled the affairs of the whole nation.

One incident still sticks in my memory. He said to me, "Frank, do you ever try to write any verses?"

I confessed that I had never been guilty of anything so base.

"Well," said he, "let's try to write some together."

I said, "All right; you begin."

In five minutes he had created a verse that I am very fond of—*Behind the Trenches of Life,* describing the wounded people about whom their friends gather to nurse them back to life.

We also wrote another poem, which, if I had anything to do with it, would have been printed many times before this, called *The Old Unteachable Kings.* Dorothy* has the

* Dorothy Doubleday Babcock, the sister of Nelson Doubleday, Sr.

only copy of it in existence, and I presume it will never be printed.

Still another subject we worked over in that little room: I suggested that he write a poem about the American Regular Army soldier. We argued for days as to what his name should be, and finally settled it as Ed Baker. The poem was begun then and completed about twenty-five years later, and is in existence today—at least, in Mr. Kipling's mind; I doubt if he has ever written it down. It is one of his best, but for some reason that I cannot fathom he will not publish it, notwithstanding that I ask him to every time I see him.

Another poem which got to the base of his brain is called *For That Was the Commodore's Way*. It refers to Mr. Noah and the Prohibitionists and is as funny a thing as I ever heard in my life. I cannot understand why he would not let it be printed; but as I have said before, the ways of authors are past finding out.

One other poem that he had in mind—which also was never put to paper, I think—was dedicated to the English merchant, and was called *The Buyer Is Always Wrong*.

One day when I went to see him he asked, "Did anybody ever call you Effendi?"

I replied, "No."

"I am going to name you Effendi after this," he said.

The reason was somewhat obvious, because my initials are F.N.D. I have tried for many years to be called Effendi only by people for whom I care and who really care for me. Thus, he did name me Effendi, which is the Turkish or Arab name for Chief, but he never called me anything but Frank in all his life.

[69]

When he was well on his road to recovery, Sam McClure called to see us one day. At that time *David Harum* was making a great success. Rud said, "Mr. McClure, have you read *David Harum?*" "No," said Sam, "why should I? The author is dead."

After pneumonia it is necessary to be careful about the heart, and I was taught by Dr. Janeway to pretty well watch Mr. Kipling's wrists. But he got steadily better, and even well enough finally to make some visits. I remember one visit in particular to the home of Mrs. Catlin, first cousin of Park & Tilford. I was invited to go along as a sort of head nurse—a job that I got quite used to.

Mr. Kipling's father, J. Lockwood Kipling, the most delightful old gentleman of seventy-five in the world, had been visiting the Catlins; and when I arrived the butler unpacked my bag and put out my clothes; and another butler came in and packed Mr. Lockwood Kipling's bag; so that when going to dress for dinner, I found that I had Mr. Kipling's clothes and he had gone with mine. As he was about forty-five inches around the waist and I was half that number of inches, you can imagine the embarrassment. There was also a difference in height of about eight inches. I did not have even shirt studs, and finally decided the whole thing was so ridiculous that I would put on Mr. Kipling's clothes, although his trousers reached only to my ankles, and go down to the dining room of these people whom I had never seen before. There was an embarrassing silence when I entered the room, but Rud's hearty laugh started the whole thing going, and it passed off with some success.

Late in the spring Kipling was well enough to go home, and as I've said, we landed him in Rottingdean quite recovered.

I had another rather trying time, so far as it concerned Mr. Kipling's health, in the fall of 1922. He had suffered for seven years from a stricture and had to go through a severe operation. As luck would have it, I was in England at that time, and again I played the part of medical errand boy.

During his convalescence our greatest form of amusement was to go to the zoo. The first day we got as far as the elephants, the second day we got as far as the snakes, and we so developed our pedestrian ability that we became very well acquainted with the animals of the zoo. Even so late as 1926 we made a visit for old times' sake to these old friends.

By a fortunate chance, my friend Christopher Morley was in London at that time. He had been very eager to meet Mr. Kipling, and I had declined about one hundred and ten thousand times to give him a letter of introduction. This presented an opportunity, and I asked Rud if he minded if I took Chris Morley along on our visit to our various animal friends, including a new pink elephant which had just arrived.

He said, "Not at all," so Christopher went with us, and I think enjoyed the occasion more than anything that had happened to him for a long time. He was very much interested in the elephant with a pink eye and a fairly white skin, and astonished to find Kipling talking Hindustani to the keeper. We secured a lot of information about our friend with the white trunk that otherwise we should not have known if Kipling had not been able to talk Hindustani, or whatever language is spoken where they grow elephants in India or Siam.

For several years Mr. and Mrs. Kipling always called Florence "Mrs. Doubleday." They became such intimate friends that this seemed to me rather ridiculous, and one day when we were all together and Mr. Kipling called her "Mrs. Doubleday," I said, "Her name is Florence." He said, "My name is Rud"; Carrie said, "My name is Caroline," and thus was overcome the embarrassment of using first names.

I never go to England to see Kipling that he does not read some new stories and tell us some new poems. It is the most maddening thing to me that some of his stories which I do not understand he prints in a book, and leaves unpublished the new verses, which I think are the best things he writes and am very anxious to see in print. I do not know if he understands himself, except that I think he has a great fear of making himself ridiculous by writing something humorous in verse. I do not know why he should feel so, because he has done it over and over with Mulvaney and all the soldier poems.

That reminds me, by the way, that he has the concluding chapter of the Mulvaney stories in his mind. He knows just what happened, but I have never been able to get it out of him and I do not think he will ever write it. I may say that Mulvaney died in this unpublished and, I believe, unwritten story. I sincerely trust that even yet Kipling will write the final act in the form of a short story. He is an exasperating chap, because he will not do what I think he ought to do. On the other hand, he expects me to do what he thinks I ought to, and I do it.

For instance, he has a new book just ready, called *Debits and Credits,* which contains the poem entitled *The Supports.* He quotes from this poem in the middle of a story in the same book, but for some reason beyond the possibility of any intelligence that I might have developed, he quotes it entirely differently. This, of course, is enough to make a proofreader wild. We telegraphed him, calling his attention to the discrepancy, and received in reply a message which simply said that the difference was intentional. How can one explain a thing like this to a proofreader? I presume our head reader, Mr. Wilcox, will die of embarrassment when we begin to receive letters from readers saying we do not know how to quote our own verse. This is an example of what publishers have to stand; they never get credit for common sense.

It is a great disappointment to me that circumstances prevent my seeing Mr. Kipling more often than I do. Somehow in all these years we have come to feel for each other things that one does not ordinarily have in one's mind or one's heart.

He had a third illness in December 1925, and Mrs. Kipling was going to send for me to help her; but I was not in good physical shape, so she did not suggest that I come. Again he went through double pneumonia, but when I saw him last in June 1926 he had entirely recovered and was his old brilliant self. Our association through all these years I trust will be a treasured heritage of my family.

This offers the only excuse for reprinting the following

letter which I recently received and which gave me vast pleasure and satisfaction:

BATEMAN'S

BURWASH

SUSSEX

Sep. 7/26

Dear Old Man:

Recent fiddlings with your wireless gift—one result of which was C. fishing up Paris, and a man there reeling off Stock Exchange quotations—has set me thinking of you more than usual and—odd though it seems—I think of you a good deal. And the day before yesterday Charles Scribner and his wife dropped in, and they both talked of you a lot. So I write to express (one doesn't do it half enough) my ancient and undeviating affection of all these many years. Also, to "constate" the fact which I don't remember that I've ever done before, that you really *are* a very big man. In a world (yours is rather worse than ours, if possible) full of alien and imported littlenesses Big men are dam' rare. I've been sitting back with a pipe and reviewing as much as I know of all you've done & made and caused to be and set in motion and inspired in your own land and outside it. ("Wonder if the man who really does things ever reckons them up in his mind. Try the experiment some day.") It seemed to me somehow that it wasn't merely the methods & manners of publishing, but the whole spirit & outlook of it, that you have revolutionized by your work *first* in the U.S. and then over here. I'm putting aside all the money & material part of it that benefitted your employees, because, after all, that is of less importance than the spiritual side.

This is one of the things that one thinks over but

[74]

generally (if one is an Englishman) doesn't set down; and now I've got it off my chest I feel more comfortable— and I hope *you* do, old man.

Ever with affection

Rud

In June 1914 we visited Kipling at Bateman's. I remember one Sunday afternoon we were sitting in the garden when Kipling turned to me and said, "Do you realize that in a few months we will be at war with Germany, and from the place where we are now sitting we shall hear the German guns from across the Channel?"

The idea seemed to me ridiculous, but Kipling appeared quite serious, and added: "If you are going to Germany, I want you particularly to notice if you see any difference in the aspect of the people—whether you see more soldiers, and whether uniforms appear to be more prominent in the streets."

We did go to Germany; we did see more uniforms; and the military people seemed to be more in authority. I was deeply impressed with this, especially as Kipling seemed so very serious, and I did the unparalleled foolish thing of telegraphing to him that England was now at liberty, so far as I was concerned, to wipe Germany off the map. It is hard to look back at that time and remember that I believed that England would have little difficulty in cleaning up Germany in a short time.

In the smoking room of a steamship which ran from Gibraltar to Algiers I once met a man who was a very great hunter. He had, I believe, killed over thirty tigers in India, and knew every place where tigers were hunted.

One day he said: "Do you know Kipling, or do you know anybody who does know him?"

I told him that I knew Kipling and he said, "I wish you would explain one thing which I never could understand." He went on to say that Kipling knew more about tigers and tiger hunting than anybody he ever knew, and he could not imagine where he had come by all this knowledge, as he never heard of his being in any tiger-infested country in India.

I told him that, so far as I knew, Kipling had never shot so much as a cat, and I was sure he had never been tiger hunting; but that he had unparalleled ability in drawing out of people any information that they had, and I was sure that he got his tiger-hunting experiences secondhand through someone who had actually shot a great many tigers. At all events, he seemed to be able to please the most fastidious critics on the subject of tiger hunting.

I had much the same experience with Kipling on my return from Germany in June 1914. He was eager to talk with me, and took me aside and questioned me about every kind of thing that I saw in Germany down to the most minute points.

I remember, also, that in 1910 I had been up in an aeroplane. Aeroplaning was unusual at that time, and he wanted to know everything about it. He had the power of dragging out of me more than I had in me and leaving me completely exhausted. This, I think, was true with everybody. I remember I introduced him to Frere Reeves,† and in half an hour, Frere told me, he got his life history

† An executive of Heinemann, a publishing company in England with which F. N. Doubleday became associated.

[76]

in a way that he had never told anybody before, and never believed that he could tell anybody. I presume this is the way that genius works.

Speaking of tigers reminds me of a young man named J. P. Kay Robinson, a nephew of Sir Perry Robinson, whom I met in England. He is a commissioner in one of the South African colonies. His nearest white neighbor is one hundred and thirty miles away and they see each other once in six months. I became acquainted with him playing golf with Robinson, and I tried to drag out of him his interesting story, with the usual difficulty. It seemed to me a very surprising thing that a man could live such a life of isolation, away from everything that was civilized, for fifteen years, as he has been doing, and be happy.

I asked him how he got to the place where his job was located, and he described it as leaving London for Southampton, taking the ship from Southampton to Capetown, taking the train from Capetown to Johannesburg, where he met a canoe with his own people and some ten or fifteen paddlers; then he went up the Zambesi River for thirty days; then walked ten days into the interior, and was home. He said he never got homesick and never got lonely—the real truth was that it was a great thing to be supreme commander. In his district he was absolute dictator, but when he got to London he was nobody.

I sent him some books, which took about six months to reach him, and he sent me as a present a lion skin which from the tip of its nose to the tip of its tail was twelve feet long. He said he started out to get this skin for me, and he came across four lions where he had expected only one. He drew a bead on the biggest one, when a fly landed on the gunsight and deliberately walked up the barrel. As he could not wait forever for it to disappear, he had to shoot; and missed the lion and nearly lost his life thereby. The second shot disabled the beast, and he eventually got him and I got the skin, which is now resting in our front hall.

In 1913 we had a delightful experience. We met Mr. and Mrs. Kipling by appointment at Wady Halfa, way up on the Nile. From there we went down the river again to Luxor, where we enjoyed ourselves for a few days. Rud was a very bad boy, much to my delight. He had received and accepted an invitation to dine with some rich people at Luxor. Much to my surprise, he suggested that we have an early dinner at the hotel, and, as it was a wonderful moonlight night, take a boat and go out on the Nile and spend the evening.

I said, "How can you do that when you have made an engagement to dine with this swell lady?"

He said, "Let me get to the telephone."

We went into the telephone booth, and he called up the lady and told her that he was very sorry to say his wife was not able to go out to dinner and he would have to cancel the engagement. I could hear a lot of sputtering at the other end, but he stuck to his point, and we did have an early dinner and stayed out until twelve o'clock and enjoyed the Nile in a way that I have never done before or since.

Even under these romantic conditions Rud and Carrie and I talked business. I suggested, or he suggested—I am not sure which—that we make a new set of Kipling which we should limit to a thousand copies, he to sign

the first volume of each set. Thus was born the Seven
Seas Edition, set in large type, and a really very beautiful
and valuable collection of books. Later on these same
plates were used by the mail-order department, and only
the other day I noticed that we were printing a new
edition of five thousand copies under the title, I think, of
the Mandalay Edition.

This is one of the reasons why our statement in August
1926 gave Kipling more income than in any six months'
period for more than twenty years. It is rather an illumi-
nating fact that our payments of royalty to Kipling have
steadily mounted in the last fifteen years, whereas everybody seems to think that his popularity is decreasing. We
will say for ourselves that we have succeeded in finding
new ways to sell the books, and have kept a steady
pressure on every title in the whole list.

It was on this trip that we made the journey up to
Khartoum after stopping awhile at Wady Halfa, made
famous by *The Four Feathers,* written by A. E. W.
Mason. Everybody who has read the book, and most
people have, will remember the jail at Omdurman where
the prisoners were so crowded that something like a third
of them were found dead every morning. Slatin Pasha
was really the hero of that story, because he was captured
by the Mahdi and was a slave to that unspeakable brute
for eleven years. The story of his escape is told in his
book, *Fire and Sword in the Soudan,* a volume of the
most exciting and vivid interest. Few people of the tourist
type went beyond Wady Halfa, and we were surprised and
delighted when we got to Khartoum to find Alice Williamson and her husband. They knew Slatin Pasha, so we were

introduced to him and invited to dinner. It seemed queer to have in Khartoum a luxurious repast served by white-robed natives, with everything most comfortable and really most modern and up to date. Slatin told us all about Omdurman and his experiences there, and he took us to see General Wingate, the Sirdar, showed us where Gordon fought and fell, and did everything he could to make our visit pleasant. He was at that time nearly sixty years old and looked like a young man of thirty-five, notwithstanding the extraordinary hardships which he endured under the Mahdi.

Slatin Pasha was an Austrian, although he served in the English Army for very many years. When the war broke out between England and Austria he was in an embarrassing position. He could not fight against his own country, and he could not bring himself to fight against the country which he had served in a military way for so many years. So he resigned his position at Khartoum, went home to Vienna, and got a job as a Red Cross official. I have not heard from him for many years, but I understood that at the age of nearly sixty, having been a bachelor all his life, he married an Austrian lady and lived happily ever after.

At Slatin's dinner party I sat next to a Major Brown, who I sensed immediately was an interesting man, and I forthwith began to dig to see if I could get any stories of his experiences, as he had lived, I think, many years in the Soudan. I did drag one tale out of him which I thought was very interesting. It seems that he was the colonel of a Soudanese regiment, and he was loud in his praises of the native Soudan soldiers, who are supposed to be the best fighters in Africa and very susceptible to

British training and influence. He had just returned from a trip far south, where he had been sent to punish a native tribe which had killed a missionary, or committed some trifling misdemeanor of that kind. So he set off with his thousand men, he as colonel, with native officers, and no other European being with him. It was a long journey south through the Sud to find this tribe, and when it was discovered, it proved to contain a larger number of natives than they had expected, and everybody in the troop realized that it would be a dangerous and possibly a long fight to administer the punishment that was necessary, which meant burning the native houses and capturing the chief conspirators.

The head officers in the regiment came to him and most respectfully explained that, he being the only white man, they dreaded going into the fight unless he would lead from the rear instead of the forefront. This made him angry, and he considered it almost treason, and he indignantly refused to be anywhere but at the head of his regiment.

When he actually came to start, the chief officers of the regiment came to him and insisted upon it that he should get off his mule and go to the rear. This he declined to do, and they removed him by force, as a result of which he had to direct the movements of the regiment from behind.

It turned out to be a much severer battle than he expected. Many of his own men were killed and many of the offending natives. When it was all over he resumed his place at the head of the regiment, so angry and upset that nothing but the shooting of the entire regiment at the moment seemed to him worth while.

"But," he said, "you must remember that I was a thousand miles or so away from Khartoum and it took a month or two to get back, during which time I began to see things in a little different light. I got back only last night," said he, "and I have not decided what I shall do about this act of treason. What would you do if you were in my place?"

I felt flattered to be asked my opinion which, of course, meant nothing, but I said: "I should shut up and say nothing more about it," which I heard afterwards he decided to do, and no action was taken. Whether his philosophy was good or bad is beyond me to express an opinion about; but I thought the subject was interesting, and as a question of discipline very important.

Later we went over to Omdurman, and a little farther up the White Nile, and saw the whole Gordon battlefield as well as the site of the Battle of Omdurman. It was as hot as blazes and required a lot of effort to go over these places, but it was one of the most interesting experiences I have ever had. I was only sorry that the Kiplings did not decide to go with us, because Khartoum itself has a perfectly good hotel and is an interesting place to see. I even went to the golf course which these English soldiers have laid out in the desert. Although there was not a blade of green grass, every shot had to be teed up in the sand. The temperature in the sun, I should think, was something like 130°, but they diligently kept at it and played every day. No people in the world are like the English for sticking to precedent; I suppose they laid out the course and began playing the second day after the Battle of Omdurman was won.

CHAPTER X

MARK TWAIN
AND HIS WAYS

THE FIRST TIME I ever met Mark Twain was in Vienna. I had just started the Doubleday & McClure business in 1897, and being in Paris and London trying to get some good authors, I heard that Mark Twain was in Vienna, so on the chance of finding him I went down there.

This was the beginning of a long friendship which was full of more experiences than I can possibly remember to relate, but I shall certainly never forget my first meeting.

I asked the clerk at the desk if I could see Mr. Samuel Clemens. He said that he did not see why I could not—that his room was number so and so and I could go right up.

I went up to the room and knocked on the door, and a stentorian voice called, "Come in!"

I entered just in time to see the tail end of a lady's nightdress disappearing into the next room. The whole place was strewn with feminine apparel. I was naturally much embarrassed and tried to withdraw, but Mark insisted upon my coming in and talking with him. He was dressed in a long nightshirt, over which he wore, most incongruously, an undershirt. When he got excited he would jump out of the bed and walk up and down the room, and Mrs. Clemens's maid would dash in at intervals and remove one or two garments and retire with her achievement. This went on until all the feminine clothing was transferred to the next room.

In the meantime Mark went on with the most droll and amusing conversation. He told me, among other things, that he had a perfect recipe for making a modern American publisher. "Take an idiot man from a lunatic asylum and marry him to an idiot woman, and the fourth generation of this connection should be a good publisher from the American point of view. I had a perfect publisher myself, as you know," he said. "His name was Frank Bliss, and thank God, he is dead and gone to hell."*

As I look back on my association with Mark Twain at that time, there was no real reason why I should not have gotten all his books and made a small fortune. It is hard to believe, but I was a little modest about interrupting his association with the brother of Frank Bliss, who, he believed, was sizzling in the flames of the Inferno.

I think the next experience I had with him was characteristic. He had invited a man named Toby, who wrote for *Punch* under the title of "Toby, M.P.," to come to visit him. After Toby had sailed from England, Mark decided to go to Italy to spend the winter, and he wrote me a letter saying that he had telegraphed Toby that I would act in his stead and be his host. As I had never seen Mr.

* Clemens himself later became a publisher.

Toby and did not care a rap for him, I confess to having been bored, but I did the best I could.

Another experience was trying to find a place for Mark to live, in which I succeeded too well. He wanted a house downtown, and one that he could walk straight through for fifty feet, as he was accustomed to get up in the night and walk in his nightclothes up and down in search of inspiration and to relieve his mind. We finally found such a house, and at his request had the lease drawn up. I was about to make a trip to Boston, but Mark was anxious that I should not go until he was established in his house. I assured him that the situation was such that he might consider himself occupying the house, and with this expression I left for Boston.

When I got home in two or three days I found that the real estate man had haunted my office, and was much distressed because Mark Twain and his family had disappeared and the lease was still unsigned.

"Give me the paper," I said, "and I will get it signed for you," as I suspected what had happened.

I went down to Ninth Street, where the house was situated, and found the sidewalk covered with old cases and packages of all kinds, and rang the bell. A servant came to the door, and I asked for Mr. Clemens, who was in the parlor.

"How do you happen to be here?" I asked.

"You said that the lease was as good as signed," he replied, "and I believed in your word, so I assumed that it was signed and moved in."

This case was a serious affair for me. Every time anything went wrong—if the stove wouldn't work, or a lock on a door got out of order—he would send for me post-haste to get it fixed. I got it fixed, and was glad when he gave up the house. His deepest resentment against the owner of the building was that this man had a very good library which he kept locked behind glass doors. Mark Twain looked upon this as an insult, which I really think it was.

One day Mark sent for me in what appeared to be great distress. Something had gone wrong with him that needed my immediate presence. I rushed down to Ninth Street to find him quite excited, and asked him what was wrong. He said he had written something that was bound to live to immortality, and he wanted to read it to me to see if it was all right. I was rather surprised to find that he was in such a hurry, and still more surprised when he told me the title, which was *The Damnation of Marie Corelli.*

It seems that the lady had arranged a reception for him after promising that he should visit her quietly and without guests, and he made up his mind to take it out on her by writing for all time his hatred of the lady and all her works. I never knew what became of it, but if it has been destroyed, it is a good job.

About this time he used to give me a great deal of advice, which was not of the type that I got from Andrew Carnegie, and frequently he would write it down. I think the best was: *Squander lies if you like, for they have no value, but husband the truth.* I hope that I have not been unduly prodigal of the truth after such advice.

Authors are strange people and have curious ideas. Mark came in one day, swore me to secrecy, and said that he had something to talk to me about which was very important; that he could tell it only to me, and I must preserve the secrecy as long as he lived.

It appears that he had written a book originally called *Selfishness,* but the title was afterwards changed to *What Is Man?* It described what selfishness meant. For instance, I remember that he considered the highest form of selfishness a mother's love for her child; she would willingly sacrifice her life, which showed her selfishness, because that was the one thing on earth which would give her satisfaction.

I thought that the whole thing was a crazy piece of business and urged him to forget it, but he thought it the best thing he had ever written, though his wife made him promise never to sign it nor to have it published in anything with which he had to do.

There was no way out of it but to have the book privately printed, which was done by De Vinne in attractive format. I think we printed two hundred and fifty copies, and he requested me to send these to two hundred and fifty distinguished men, asking them what they thought of it, his name, of course, not being divulged to anybody. This seemed to me a fool business which I was very loath to do; but I did send it, as he requested, to over two hundred of the most distinguished men in the United States, mostly literary people.

If I remember rightly, I got two replies; one from J. Lockwood Kipling, who wrote that the author's argument was so obviously correct that it was not worth discussing; the other from Andrew Carnegie, who simply acknowledged it as a book and then wrote about other things.

The disappointment of Mark was intense. He and his

wife apparently thought that the publication would make a great sensation. I do not know what eventually became of the book, though I think it was finally published with Mark's name on it. It was, I always thought, a poor thing, and I think so yet.

One day when I was very busy and we were still occupying very small quarters on Sixteenth Street and Union Square, Mark Twain drifted in, smoking a cigar that could be smelled a mile. He insisted upon it that it was a good cigar because he paid seven dollars a barrel for them; but with this I did not agree.

He asked me if I was busy, and I told him that I was. He said to go right on with my work and he would make himself at home for a few minutes.

He certainly did. In less time than it takes to write about it almost, he filled the room with a blue smoke, nauseating in its effect, and then he began to look around among the volumes on the shelves. I had in this office some special books which I was carefully keeping for one purpose or another. Mark went around and found a book he wanted, took out a pencil and wrote on the flyleaf, *To my friend, Samuel L. Clemens, with the kind regards of F. N. Doubleday,* put it under his arm, and disappeared.

At the time I failed to realize what a good joke it was. As I look back on it now, it is all right.

He was a constant visitor; although I had no business with him, he used to drop in just to smoke those seven-dollar-a-barrel cigars, which must have killed every insect that was in the neighborhood. One day I was not able to go to luncheon on Sixteenth Street where we had our house, and Mark turned up about half past two or three o'clock in the afternoon. He just stuck his head in the door to say, "I only called to tell you that you had better not go home to lunch, because there won't be any lunch."

I asked him what was the matter. He said that he had been over to lunch and eaten up everything. It was his custom not to take any lunch, but he said that when he did fall he ate everything in sight; so he warned me not to rely on any food for luncheon, and passed out of the door, leaving a trail of pungent smoke.

CHAPTER XI

DOUBLEDAY, PAGE & COMPANY
AND WALTER H. PAGE

Toward the end of 1899 Sam McClure and I, I am sorry to say, had a disagreement. There was no personal feeling about it, but we simply could not agree. He had regarded with great feeling what he thought was our non-success in carrying off the Harper deal. I confessed to being not so large-minded and to being glad to be out of the whole Harper imbroglio. Sam hoped at all times that he might find another opportunity to go back and take charge of the Harper business, but I was bound that it should not happen.

So it came about that Sam suggested that we should combine the S. S. McClure Company and Doubleday & McClure Company. As this would have taken the control out of my hands, I was not willing to do it. We agreed to separate. The parting was most amicable, with no feeling on either side except friendliness; but I was determined not to leave the control in the hands of anybody but myself, especially not to Sam, for whom I had a great affection, but whose judgment, I thought, was very poor.

On December 31, 1899, therefore, I purchased the assets of the Doubleday & McClure Company, paid Mr. McClure forty-nine per cent of the profits that we had earned, and made some arrangement for taking over the books on terms satisfactory to him and to myself. On the first of January 1900 we started on the new deal.

Mr. McClure had been to see Walter Hines Page, who was at that time editor of the *Atlantic Monthly,* and had induced him to give up his job, with many flamboyant predictions to the effect that we would have to deal with eight or ten periodicals to be published by Harper's, whom we expected to control, and that we would make a great encyclopedia which would make the *Encyclopaedia Britannica* look like a pamphlet. All this was done without any consultation with me, and the first thing I knew Walter Page moved into the office and began to work on the encyclopedia plan on a basis that was truly gigantic. It did not take me long to appreciate that this would be a matter of financial life and death, mostly the latter. The cost of producing the set would have been at least a million dollars, and we did not have the money handy around the house.

Page also worried about this. The Harper scheme had fallen through and he found himself rather in the position of having disassociated himself from his old job and not having a very strong hold on a new job which was worthy of his best efforts.

He came to me and talked it over, and suggested that

he leave the McClure Company and join our company, and that the firm should be called Doubleday, Page & Company. I had had a long experience with Page and had much affection for him, and we were very glad to have him become one of us; so the new firm of Doubleday, Page & Company was started, with Page as vice-president, John Leslie Thompson as treasurer, William Henry Lanier as secretary, and your humble servant as president.

Truly the starting of Doubleday, Page & Company was very different from the starting of Doubleday & McClure Company. After three years of existence we had a list of some value; we had an organization of even greater value; we had a bank account sufficiently large to take advantage of all cash discounts; and a credit at the Chemical National Bank which provided comfortably for what we needed in the way of cash. This was the reverse in almost all respects of the situation when we started the old firm.

We moved from the Power House on Lexington Avenue to 34 Union Square. Here we had a floor, I think about one hundred feet long and twenty-five feet wide, big enough for our needs. Sometimes I wonder how such a small space could have contained so much enthusiasm and so many schemes. We bristled with ideas; some of them were pretty good.

I have often thought, for example, that we must have had real courage when we started the Nature Library,* because these books were expensive and required an investment of anywhere from three to five thousand dollars

---

* Neltje De Graff, F.N.D.'s first wife, wrote several of the books published in the Nature Library, under the pen name of Neltje Blanchan.

to make the plates. Eventually it became one of our best sellers and was a foundation stone in our business.

It was not long before Page began to worry to get his fingers in a magazine, and *The World's Work* resulted. I, too, had some of the same sensations, and so, besides *The World's Work,* before we had been in the book business two years we started *Country Life in America.* From my point of view, *The World's Work* was a success from the start. I think the first year we may have lost four or five thousand dollars, but if anybody would take the trouble to look back and read the contents of the first six numbers, I am sure he would be surprised that we do so badly by comparison today, particularly in mechanical make-up.

Page was a delightful man to work with. Most editors are very reserved; he was very large-minded, was always open to ideas, and besought anybody who had an idea to give it to him. His patience in listening to bores was beyond expression. His attitude was the reverse of that of most editors. When anyone came into his office, bore or genius, Page treated him like a long-lost friend who had some valuable information to impart. I do not know that he got enough help in return for the enormous amount of time he spent; but he certainly showed a quality of mind and heart which is pleasant to think of.

I think it was twelve months after *The World's Work* was started that we published the first number of *Country Life in America,* and this succeeded even more quickly; the risk was less and the opportunities quite as large, although the circulation was much smaller.

I must give great credit, too, to Harry Lanier, who acted

as art editor for both magazines, as well as editor of our book department, and encompassed an amount of work which was simply appalling. Later his health broke down and he left us. I am glad to hear that he is recovered and is now the editor of a most successful magazine, the *Golden Book*.

One unfortunate experience was with J. L. Thompson, who was the head of the sales department and had charge also of our small monetary affairs. When Mr. Carnegie told me that we were foolish not to have a monthly statement, we all put it up to Thompson to work out; but he either could not or would not, and we felt that we had to make a change in order that this great foundational feature should be established in our business. He went to Scribner, and I hope succeeded there.

Mr. Samuel A. Everitt, who had been with us almost from the first, took Mr. Thompson's place as treasurer of the company, and worked out the plans which we all thought were necessary to the success of the financial side of the business.

Many other efficient helpers took part in this constructive work. I think I am safe in saying that we established then a feeling of friendliness and extraordinary co-operation which personally I think has been largely responsible for what success we have made.

Among Page's manifold duties was the reading of certain manuscripts, which I never thought he particularly enjoyed. One experience looked at the time rather serious, but it came out all right. Some gentleman who lived, I think, in Chicago, sent Page a manuscript—I believe, of a novel. Page acknowledged its receipt, and it simply disappeared from the face of the earth; there was no trace of it in any department. After some weeks he was obliged to confess that the manuscript was lost and we did not see any chance of ever finding it. Page, in his capacity as a letter writer, could do almost anything with the pen when he started out; and he wrote to the gentleman apologizing for our carelessness and asked him what he would like to have us do.

The author simply telegraphed: "The manuscript was no damn good, anyway. Forget it."

Within a day or two a lady walked into the office and put a manuscript on Mr. Page's desk and said: "You gave me this manuscript to read and I had forgotten that I had it. Here it is, and it is no good." So all was well.

This, I am sorry to say, happened once in our house. A manuscript was sent to Oyster Bay and put in a closet by a servant, and left there for months. But so far as I know, these are the only two cases in which we had such hard luck.

In 1913 Mr. Woodrow Wilson asked Walter Page to go to London as American ambassador.† It is not for me to say, but I think he was not very enthusiastic for the job; but he had exactly the characteristics of a successful ambassador, and, as everybody knows, was successful from the first. O. Henry once said of him that he could take a Page letter declining a manuscript and cash it at any bank. It would be only presumptuous for me to attempt to write any history of his career so far as he was associated with

† Mr. Doubleday wrote, in another version of his recollections: "In 1913 [Page] went to Europe as American ambassador to London, having resigned his association with us, very much to our regret."

me, since his *Life and Letters,* and especially his own letters, tell the story with such extraordinary interest and effectiveness.

As his term of office as ambassador drew to a close, we developed plans for the future. Some of these were expressed in letters which appeared in the book, and others, I think, have only found a record in my own inadequate brain; but I know that if he had lived and come back in full vigor, as we hoped, many things would have been accomplished, and some things, I trust, for the public good. But that was not to be.

I think Page was very much delighted with the Garden City idea;‡ it appealed to him, and as soon as the place was built, he moved down and took a house in Garden City, where he spent much of his time and did much of his editorial work.

I remember his inviting the General Education Board to luncheon. He showed them around the place and took a genuine pride in the grounds. Many and many is the time he wrote to us, during the days of stress in England during the war, that he was homesick for our Garden City enterprise. I can never cease to regret that he was not able when he came back to come down and see how the place had changed, and I hope and believe very much improved.

‡ Doubleday's offices and printing plant on Long Island, built in 1910.

CHAPTER XII

CONDUCTING THE PUBLISHING BUSINESS OF A RIVAL

Much to my regret, my two old friends, Sam McClure and John S. Phillips, who, after the separation of the Doubleday & McClure Company from the S. S. Mc-Clure Company, were running the S. S. McClure Company, publishers of *McClure's Magazine,* and McClure, Phillips & Company, publishers of books, fell out. Without any warning, so far as I know, Mr. Phillips resigned the vice-presidency of both these companies, took with him most of the staff, and bought an interest in the *American Magazine.* This left Sam as helpless as a drooling infant. He could run the business and editorial organization of a publication about as well as a slightly older baby with two teeth could eat beefsteak, and I remember his helpless attitude when he came to me and told me the story.

He was very anxious that I should come in and be a partner in John Phillips's place. This I was unwilling to do, because I had to consider my loyalty toward our own publishing house, and, to speak the honest truth, I did not want to get wound up again with Sam and all his visionary ideas. I declined the invitation, I think, about three times. One night he appeared at Locust Valley and sat up telling me his troubles until the midnight hours, with the result that I promised to be one of five directors, and felt very sorry for myself, as well as for Sam.

The next day I went off carefully on a three days' golfing expedition. When I got back I found waiting at my office door Michael Flynn, the cashier and confidential man of the McClure business, whose hands were full of important-looking papers, checks, and all sorts of possible trouble.

I asked him what I could do for him. He said, "I would like to get you to sign these papers, including the checks for the payroll."

"What have I got to do with it?" I asked.

"Didn't you know," he replied, "that you were elected managing director of the McClure Company?"

I told him that I had agreed to be one of five directors, but he said, "They held a meeting, and all the authority has been given to you; I want to get these checks signed, and make an arrangement with you so that we can go on with the business."

This was a fearful blow, and I confess I was a little angry. I said, "Tell Mr. McClure that I won't do it."

Flynn said, "I can't very well do that, because he has been on the ocean two days. He sailed immediately on your election."

Here I was in the most awful situation. If I fulfilled faithfully my job as managing director of the McClure

Company, I did not know how I could fulfill it faithfully as president of Doubleday, Page & Company, who were rivals in every department.

I finally decided that I would carry on until I could get Sam back and relieve myself of this situation. Sam was too smart for me; he refused to come back, and for six months I conducted the business of three publishing concerns—the S. S. McClure Company, the McClure Company (which the book publishing business was now called), and Doubleday, Page & Company. Everybody helped and things went on swimmingly. I cannot at the moment remember how much money we made, but the whole McClure enterprise was lifted out of the slough of despond into a profitable affair. This was not due to any cleverness on my part; the truth really was that they had a splendid list of books and a popular and successful magazine, and all we had to do was to prevent Mr. McClure from throwing the money out of the window as soon as he achieved a fair amount of success.

At last, at the end of six months when I got Mr. McClure to return, his business was in good shape; he owed little or no money, and was in a position to go on under most favorable conditions. He expressed himself as deeply grateful, and for some reason wanted to give me a check for eighteen thousand dollars. This I declined; I told him that I had not undertaken the job for money, and to introduce it into the subject would not please me. He asked if there was not some way in which he could show his appreciation, and I told him that there was— that I would regard it as a great favor and would be highly delighted if he would not throw away this money which we had accumulated, or do foolish things which might injure the business—if he were willing to consult me before he made any vital change, I should be abundantly repaid for any trouble I had had.

This he faithfully promised to do, and within three months he got the business so involved with a number of crooks who picked him up that it never really recovered again. As rivals of ours, this may have been a good thing for us, but it was a bad thing for publishing, and we all deeply regretted the loss of Sam's money and position. I do not know but that a publisher of the type of Sam McClure is very much like unreliable authors who do queer things.

One more tale I must tell of Sam before I close the story of our association. I met him on Fifth Avenue one day, and casually mentioned the fact that I was going to Europe the next morning.

"I am glad you spoke of it," he said. "I think I will go with you." And, sure enough, there he was at the gangplank when we sailed for Liverpool.

Two or three nights out of the port of New York I gave a dinner party, I think of twelve or fourteen people, including Sam McClure and his wife. Sam got very much excited because the band played music which he thought was inappropriate—what was the equivalent of jazz nowadays. He went to the leader of the orchestra and prevailed on him to introduce some new numbers, and when they finally began to play Wagner, Sam rose from his chair to drink the health of the great musician and said: "Ah, Wagner! He was the McClure of music."

Whether there was an element of humor in this toast, I will not say; at all events, it happened, and I am inclined to believe represented the inside of Sam's mind concerning himself.

CHAPTER XIII

THE MOVE
TO SIXTEENTH STREET
AND STRIKES

At the beginning of the century we found ourselves a very happy and congenial family at number 34 Union Square. I remember very well that when we took this floor we thought it would last us for a year or two at least; but we instantly began to be crowded, and had to add two floors to our lease. Even then we were unbearably cramped for space.

One rather interesting thing we did on the top floor. A man named H. M. O'Brien came to see us one time and asked us why we did not start our own plant. As our output was very small, this did not seem to look particularly practical, but we hired O'Brien to set advertisements and to do work in association with the printers who made *The World's Work,* and gradually developed a little composing room which was really the start of the Country Life Press.

Our business continued to grow prosperously, and we were obliged to have our work done in various parts of the city; even some of our offices were crowded out of Union Square, and we were faced with the necessity of moving to a new place, which resulted eventually in our putting up a building of six stories containing perhaps thirty thousand feet of floor space on Sixteenth Street near Irving Place. We were inexperienced in building matters and had a horrible time dealing with a fly-by-night builder who was supposed to put up capital and produce the building ready for our occupancy. Nothing of the sort happened. The only way that we finally did complete the building was to put up the money ourselves, complicated by all sorts of curious relations with this builder and the lawyer who was lending him money and was involved in other building enterprises.

However, we finally completed the building, which seemed enormous. I remember the rent amounted to something over ten thousand dollars a year; we all thought we were taking a tremendous risk. Anyhow, we moved in, purchased the equipment to print our magazines, and began business in the new quarters in the fall of 1904.

When I think of this building I am always reminded of one particular incident. In 1908, I think it was, we had a strike. The question arose whether we should be allowed to run an open shop or must conduct a closed union shop. We felt very strongly on this subject of the open shop and decided to fight. The unions notified us that they would strike on the first of January. We had the misfortune to associate ourselves with all the other printers in the city, who had decided to resist the demands of the union. I never want to go in co-operation with another group of men to fight a strike. In my opinion, it is twice as easy to do it by yourself, for the reason that you are only as strong as the weakest member, and the weakest member of such an organization is pretty weak.

However, to make a painful story not so painfully long, we won the strike, I think largely because we did not know how to fight a strike and our methods were new and original, and the union did not know exactly how to meet our schemes.

I was very much surprised to learn that the employers planned to bring in their men to take the place of the strikers on Monday morning, although the compositors left Friday night. It occurred to us that we would organize our force and induce them to go to work Saturday morning before the pickets got onto it. This we did, bringing in from the country some fifteen or twenty men, who were glad of an opportunity to get a job in the city at high wages and in an open shop. We got them into the building Saturday morning when there were no pickets and there was a more or less quiet spell. We found that the old hands before leaving had pied the type and raised hob with the material in the composing room. This we put our men at work on, and by Monday morning, when the strike really took official form, we were beginning to produce something in the way of composition.

I think we did better than any of our associates in getting over the strike quickly. When we got going, everybody expected that we would give our men to other people not so well off, and in some cases we did; but this illustrates the point I wish to make: that I would rather fight a strike alone than with many or few associates.

For months and almost years our building had to be

protected by policemen. We lived within a few blocks of the office, and whenever there was trouble they would come to the house; and strikes, police, and miscellaneous troubles were all mixed up together. One night when the night shift was running the presses two union pickets broke in the door and started to put emery in some of the machinery. Two girls from the bindery were coming down the stairs at the time and they were attacked by the pickets; but fortunately a policeman was in the building, and he took both men off to jail.

We thought that this was a good chance to make an example, and we hoped that it would have an influence on the union. When the case came up for trial, an Irish judge was on the bench and we had trouble in holding our prisoners; but we employed an Irish judge-lawyer to prosecute the case, and they were released on bail with the understanding that the case was to be tried by a higher court than the one to which they were originally taken. The prisoners jumped bail and the union had to forfeit a thousand dollars apiece; I think it took us about two years of detective work to catch these fellows and rearrest them. Finally we succeeded and brought them to trial, and they were convicted or put on parole, I do not know which. But the union had a lesson, and as long as we were on Sixteenth Street they never bothered us again.

I have not forgotten our interview with the union leaders. They said that if we would stop the prosecution of these two men they would agree to leave us alone. We told them on the contrary—that we had been fighting the strike now for over a year and we had got the strike-fighting habit and did not want to give it up. Perhaps this had some influence on their feeling that it was not worth while to fight us.

From this distance it all sounds rather tame, but I confess that I was frightened to death when the strike actually began—so frightened, indeed, that I was afraid to lie down.

We had a strong person in O'Brien, an Irishman who was afraid of nothing whatever, and his moral effect was of inestimable value. It was a great pity that he was not a bigger man, because when the plant grew to large proportions he was unable to grow with it, but he is still on the payroll.

While we are on the subject, as we had only one other severe strike, we might as well continue the story.

When we moved down to Garden City, we took with us the men who filled the key positions, or at least as many of them as we could, and developed our organization of new men from this start. We had union men and non-union men, inexperienced men and experienced men—rather a good crowd on the whole. But the union got after us in 1913 and again demanded a closed union shop. Through the union delegates, they succeeded in enrolling about half of our men who had come in as independent workers, and when the time was ripe these men were pulled out, leaving us crippled in every department. However, there was never for a moment any idea of giving up, and we immediately hired guards to protect our people, and fought the fight to a successful conclusion in a few months—a very expensive luxury, but absolutely needed if one is going to keep one's independence.

If I were a writer, I should like to discuss the question of capital and labor as I have observed it, and to upset some of the old theories, if it is possible to upset them. Although I think the attitude of the employer is much better than it was, I am inclined to blame the employer very largely for many of the troubles into which he falls. Until recently the average man who hired labor of any kind regarded a low salary as a profitable one to the capitalist, whereas the whole country is now pretty well convinced that this is not true.

We have run an open shop, or what practically amounts to a closed shop with the key inside, from that day to this. We have, I hope, paid our men more than they could earn elsewhere, and they on their part have produced more than is produced by other people in the same line. They have been given good working conditions and our turnover is almost nil: indeed, it has become one of our troubles that so few of our people resign that the younger employees are held back because of the lack of opportunity which arises except by increasing the force.

You will hear people talk a great deal of how working people are not appreciative of good conditions and good treatment. We have not found this to be true. I think there is no question, for instance, that the average employee throughout the building appreciates and cares for the gardens and the attractions which we try to add to the beauty of the place.

In 1913 when we had this very severe strike which, as I say, involved every process of book and magazine making, the plant was, as usual, picketed. I presume there were eight or ten men walking up and down in front of the building. Mr. Everitt and I used to go out in the morning, gather a few flowers from the garden, and pin them on the pickets with the words, "We will pin a rose on you." It may be my imagination, but I like to think that this cheerful philosophy had a real influence in making these men feel sheepish; at all events, they soon dropped off, and gradually the whole strike enterprise came to an end, and we had an organization which I think was as faithful and efficient as any ever brought together. At any rate, they have created large profits and I hope have been well rewarded themselves. As we have some two or three hundred stockholders in the building who have received an average dividend of eighteen per cent on their preferred stock, it looks as if they were satisfied.

The stockholder-employee is another subject which might be written about at great length and immense tiresomeness, but I will not go into it except to say that, so far as I can see, the selling of certain preferred stocks to our own employees has been uniformly successful. We have never sold enough to satisfy the demand, which I think is a strong point. Our men have not only paid for the stock but have saved money besides. To encourage them to save, we pay into the savings bank an amount equal to the interest which the bank allows, and I think at all times the Nassau County Trust Company has savings to the amount of nearly one hundred thousand dollars in its hands, which shows prosperity as well as thrift.

Another subject which interests me very much and which I wish I had more figures on is the benefit of moving out of New York City. I cannot tell exactly how many hours our people consumed in getting to their work when our place was on Sixteenth Street, New York, but in London* it was something like two hours and twenty minutes a day on the average for the round trip, and at considerable and increasing expense. Practically all of our people are within half an hour or less of Country Life Press, and this saving of money and time and temper must in the end be a very large influence. The whole subject of moving any plant that manufactures goods out of the city of New York or any other big center is one of terrifically growing importance. Personally, I am glad that we began as far back as we did.

Talking about strikes—we had another experience which was quite upsetting.

As a war duty, we created and managed for the Red Cross Association the *Red Cross Magazine*. It attained a circulation of more than a million, and I should think that the advertising yielded for the Red Cross more than a million dollars. I was put in charge by Harry Davison, who headed the Red Cross Association.

With the idea of being very careful, I gave the printing to three houses: one non-union shop, one union shop, and one open shop, and thought I had pretty well covered any criticism which might arise. The Lord knows, there was plenty of criticism about everything at that time, and everything done in any department in connection with the war was examined with the utmost care and often with distinct hostility.

One day I received a telegram from Harry Davison, who wished me to come to Washington at once, because

* Mr. Doubleday was referring to William Heinemann, Ltd., which he bought in 1921. F.N.D. was largely responsible for the plant at Kingswood, Surrey, a pioneering move to "the country."

they had struck a serious snag. It appeared that old man Gompers† and his crew had discovered that part of the work of printing the magazine was done at Donnelley's in Chicago, which was a non-union shop, and part at Country Life Press. He demanded that both Donnelley and ourselves, because we printed the *Red Cross Magazine,* should be turned into closed union shops.

I was in an embarrassing position and told Davison that I would be quite willing to drop out and let someone take my place and he could print the magazine wherever he chose; but I could not change our open shop to a closed shop for anybody under any circumstances.

They put pressure on me to do this, because they were satisfied that they were making money out of the magazine and they did not want to take it out of our hands; yet they were afraid of Gompers, who threatened to spoil their next money drive.

Finally they induced ex-President Taft to come in and talk with Gompers, and explain that if they took the magazine away they would lose our assistance, which was very valuable to them at the time, because we would not give up our principle of the open shop. Taft was clever enough to explain to Gompers that he would do his union more harm than good if he spoiled a drive for any such reason as this, so the thing finally passed over. Personally, I was anxious to get rid of the responsibility of the *Red Cross Magazine,* and eventually it served its purpose and died a natural death.

Though there have been several rather trying experiences

† Samuel Gompers, an early labor leader.

in connection with running an open shop, I remember one which was certainly gratifying.

The union over and over again has tried to get employed in Country Life Press men who would influence the workers to join the union. At one time an old friend of one of the foremen came to him and said he wanted a job. As a man of that particular caliber was needed at that particular time, the fellow was taken in and went to work. I think he had been in our employ perhaps six months when he went to the foreman and said that he wished to be fired. The foreman said there was no reason for his being fired, because he was doing very good work—why should he suggest it?

Finally, under the seal of the deepest secrecy, he told the foreman that he had come in as an emissary from the union to try to wean the men away from the open shop and to help establish union control. The first thing that happened to him was that he got sick, and the nurse took care of him. Then his wife got sick and we again took care of her; and four or five things of this sort happened, which made him thoroughly ashamed to be a traitor in a camp which had treated him so kindly. He said, too, that he could not bring himself to make trouble in an organization so happy and prosperous.

We finally had to let him go, as he was too much wound up with union circles to be able really to feel like a free man.

CHAPTER XIV

THE VALUE
OF A LIST

In 1908 Mr. McClure offered to sell us the McClure book business. We were having a hard enough time to keep up our sales, as our list was small and our expenses were high. This offered us an opportunity which we immediately accepted, and began negotiations which came to a successful conclusion.

We worked out a plan to liquidate the business in such a way that McClure would have most of the profits in the beginning and we would own the business in the end. We had planned to pay him so much a month—if I remember rightly, ten or fifteen thousand dollars—the whole sum involved being between one hundred and one hundred and fifty thousand dollars. We gave him notes for this money, promising to clear up the whole thing within a year. He was always to offer these notes to us for redemption before selling them to a bank or otherwise disposing of them. I think that he offered them all to us within sixty days, which made quite a strain on our finances; but we managed with the help of bank loans to take up all of these notes, and we found ourselves possessed of all the assets of the McClure book business, including authors, plates, rights, trade accounts, stock, and everything else.

Really this was one of the most fortunate things that ever happened to us. Thus came into our possession the list and the business which four or five years previously I had run for Mr. McClure when he went to Europe and was left high and dry by his partners, Mr. Phillips, Mr. Brady, et al.

The effect on our business was instantaneous. The addition to our list was, as one can easily see, of the utmost value. The purchase of a publishing business with a substantial collection of plates proved to be among the most successful enterprises we have ever identified with, both in this case of McClure and in the later case of Heinemann in England. In the old days the Houghton Mifflin Company built up their business by buying out two or three Boston publishers. So far as I can see, it is the quickest and most surely successful method of developing a fine business, but unfortunately publishing house assets do not often come into the market.

The success which followed taking over the McClure list is easily accounted for when one considers that we found ourselves in possession of authors like the following:

Conrad, who had not then begun to be well known, but whose development is told of in another chapter. This alone was worth thousands of dollars not only in money but in prestige, as it turned out.

Edwin Markham's poems were a helpful item. *The Man*

[113]

with the Hoe was famous and very successful for many years, and still is.

Booth Tarkington had a tremendous value. The McClure list contained most of his books at that time, among them *The Gentleman from Indiana, Monsieur Beaucaire, In the Arena, The Beautiful Lady,* etc. It gave us an established connection with Tarkington which unfortunately had been broken, but which was now restored.

Conan Doyle, with *The Return of Sherlock Holmes* and *The Hound of the Baskervilles,* came to us when he was most popular and very valuable.

Stewart Edward White, with his long list, was among the most important of the additions.

The Life of Pasteur has been a little gold mine in itself, and in the last two or three years has sold upwards of fifty or sixty thousand copies.

Kate Douglas Wiggin's Crimson Classics turned out to be a set of great value and is sold in many departments in many ways; and will be sold for years to come as the result of new ideas which we will develop.

O. Henry's books alone would almost have been worth the whole price of admission.

The Williamsons,* whose *Lightning Conductor* had just been a great success, were most popular at the time of purchase.

Joel Chandler Harris, represented with *Told by Uncle Remus* and several other books, was another famous author. Unfortunately, he died soon after the books were taken over, but to have his books at all was valuable.

---

* Charles Norris Williamson and his wife Alice Muriel (nee Livingston).

Anthony Hope Hawkins was also popular at the time. And so we could go on with dozens of authors and dozens of books.

One other experience we had in this line. In 1912 we took over the publication department of the Baker & Taylor Company; but this was essentially a jobbing house and its publishing department never was much of a success. I think we probably lost money on this list, but it brought us into close association with the Baker & Taylor Company—an intimacy which has endured until today, and I am sure has been to our advantage and I hope to theirs, since they are men of character and attainments and most agreeable people with whom to work.

CHAPTER XV

THE MYSTERY
OF "O. HENRY"

AMONG other things, the inventory of the McClure book business included contracts for most of the books of Sydney Porter, or "O. Henry," as he was known then.

The McClure Company had purchased for five hundred dollars the complete rights in each of the O. Henry books. As the sales were not large, I presume the money represented a reasonable price. O. Henry himself was rather distressed not to have any interest in the books and their possible future sale, which might be of benefit to his family. We were very glad to restore his rights and to give him a royalty.

One day I saw Mr. Charles D. Lanier, who had a subscription book business in connection with the *Review of Reviews*. He was a good customer of ours and bought millions of books from us, mostly for sale in association with the magazine. I suggested that he should sell a set of O. Henry in twelve volumes. The idea, he said, was absurd—nobody would buy a collection of short stories.

But I argued that O. Henry had a following, if not large, at least distinguished, and that we had just published a Manuscript Edition of his works for one hundred and twenty-five dollars a set, and sold every copy of it immediately. I outlined an advertisement for him which would call attention to the fact that the same reading matter was available with a subscription to the *Review of Reviews* for one fifth, or one tenth the price that these people had paid.

After a long time I induced him to take it up and try it, which he did with enormous success. I think that the *Review of Reviews* sold something more than four hundred and fifty thousand sets, and the books are selling today in great numbers. For instance, we have just sold one hundred thousand copies of the complete works of O. Henry in one volume to the Funk & Wagnalls Company, to be sold in connection with the *Literary Digest*. This is nearly twenty years after the purchase of the books with the McClure list and shows the surprising vitality of the property.

O. Henry himself died and left almost nothing except these books. They have, I hope, supported the family ever since.

Some time after his death, we found that he had sold the dramatic rights in all of his stories to Mr. George C. Tyler for five hundred dollars. These Mr. Tyler permitted us to repurchase at a reasonable price, and they have since been administered for the benefit of the estate.

O. Henry certainly had a sense of humor, and one instance always amuses me when I think of it. There was a young man who published a magazine called *Hampton's*. He was very anxious to purchase a short story from

O. Henry, and was willing to pay, he said, five hundred dollars. Hampton did not trust O. Henry, and O. Henry did not trust Hampton. O. Henry wanted Hampton to pay his five hundred dollars in advance, and Hampton wanted O. Henry to give him the manuscript to read before he paid the money.

They came to a deadlock. Finally Hampton suggested that O. Henry give him half of the story and he would pay him two hundred and fifty dollars on delivery, and the other two hundred and fifty as soon as the other half was delivered. So O. Henry handed the incomplete story to Hampton, with the request that he should read it and send a check for the rest of the money due.

Time went on and no check came. Hampton would not answer letters. The mystery was explained about two months later when Hampton published the half of the story which O. Henry had written, with an offer of a two-hundred-and-fifty-dollar prize to anybody who would complete it. I believe O. Henry never did get the other two hundred and fifty dollars.

He had a habit of coming into the office about five o'clock in the afternoon when the cashier was just going home, and insisting upon having twenty-five or fifty dollars. We could not imagine why he was under such a stress —we knew that he was hard up, but why he had to have money at the end of an afternoon in a few minutes was a mystery for a long time.

It turned out later that Al Jennings, who knew him in Central America, had instituted a series of blackmailing enterprises, on the ground that if O. Henry did not give him twenty-five dollars that night he would tell everybody that he had been to jail, etc.

It was a pathetic thing. Porter was of a very nervous temperament, and I am sure this wear and tear had a corrosive influence on his physical condition and helped to cause his pitifully early death.

I did not know Porter very well; he was one of the shyest men I ever met. He was always dreadfully hard up for money, and his tragic story has been told by his biographer, Dr. C. Alphonso Smith.*

* And, more recently, by Richard O'Connor in *O. Henry, The Legendary Life of William S. Porter,* published in 1970.

CHAPTER XVI

A GOOD JOB
WELL DONE

THESE secret memoirs have been full of what our friends did for us. There was one thing that we did for a friend for which I think we can take credit. If it sounds egotistical, let it go at that, because it was the result of a combination of effort in which all our partners shared.

I speak of our association with an author named Conrad. It really began in 1908 when we purchased the McClure book business, but there is a story before this which I must tell.

The first year that I was in business for myself I went to see William Heinemann in London. Heinemann had a great flair for a new literary light. I told him that I was just starting in business, and asked him if he knew a future Kipling.

"I can tell you of at least one," he said. "They call him Joseph Conrad, because he has an impossible Polish name, Josef Teodor Konrad Nalecz Korzeniowski, and he is almost starving to death. He has written two or three books which have been entirely unsuccessful, and he can't get enough money to keep body and soul together until he can write some more. He is at present writing a novel called *The Rescue,* but he hasn't enough money to live on until it is finished. If you would like to contribute fifty dollars a month, I will advance an equal amount, and he will be provided with the means to get this job done. I am sure it will pay its way, though I have no great expectation of a large sale."

Fifty dollars a month seemed to me at that time an awful lot of money, but I agreed to do it, and for a year or two Heinemann and we contributed this sum, which Conrad used to keep going while he wrote *The Rescue.*

At the end of that time I received a letter from Conrad saying that the book would not come off and he could not finish it. He was very sorry, and he would give us what there was of it, in the hope that someday he could come back and complete it. I read with the utmost pleasure and appreciation the chapters which were already written. I thought them very, very fine, but as he could not go any further, there was nothing to be done, and the manuscript was tucked away—I had no idea what became of it.

After twenty years, during which a lot of things happened, I received a letter from Conrad in which he said that he had now found a way to complete *The Rescue,* and he was immediately going to work to do it.

So it fell out that twenty years later this famous novel was completed, and nobody can tell where the old part ended and the new began. It was, I think, as good as anything he ever wrote, and when published sold fifty thousand copies, which was at that time an unheard-of sale for Conrad.

But to go back for a minute to what I claim we did for the Conrad property, and, so far as I am concerned, how it came about:

One day Mrs. Winslow S. Pierce, of Bayville, said to me that she had been reading a really great book called *Lord Jim,* by Joseph Conrad. I had not read the book or thought much about it; but I was impressed with what she said and, hunting it up, found that it was one of the five books that we purchased from the McClure Company when we took over that business. I immediately read it and was much impressed by it, and the conviction came to my mind that in Conrad we had a great author, although not one of his books had sold, I think, above two thousand copies.

My partners agreed with me that we should get into our own hands all the Conrad books published, although they probably would not pay for the cost of the plates. I remember that I went to Dodd, Mead & Company and asked them if they would sell *The Nigger of the Narcissus,* and they said, "Gladly." I bought it for two hundred and fifty dollars. I had the same experience with Putnam's in the case of *Typhoon,* with Appleton on *An Outcast of the Islands,* with Macmillan on *Almayer's Folly,* and with Scribner's in the case of *Tales of Unrest.* The only books outstanding which I could not get were published by Harper's, who were in a financial state which did not permit them to transfer copyrights, or so I understood.

So here we had Conrad and most of his books, with very few sales.

In 1912, I think, Conrad wrote and put into the hands of James B. Pinker, his literary agent, a book called *Chance*. George Doran* happened to be in London at the time, and took over the contract for the publication of the book, with a small advance and a reasonable royalty. We were much distressed at this, because we had counted on having all of his other books; but Conrad and Pinker, it seemed, had the impression that we had lost enough money on the Conrad books and that we would not like to continue.

I went frankly to Doran and told him the whole story —that we had this ambition to make Conrad successful, and we controlled most of his volumes. He was extremely good and said that, if we would refund him the advance, he would transfer the book to us, which he did, along with *'Twixt Land and Sea,* the publishing rights of which he had secured at the same time.

If I am any judge of books, *Chance* was the hardest of all the Conrad books to read. I should have said it was the most unlikely book to make a success with the public of all his long list. But it shows how little one knows, because the critics as well as readers took up *Chance* as they had not done with any other of the Conrad volumes. It was quite a success and I think we sold eight or ten thousand copies, which was astonishing for Conrad at that time.

This was the beginning of his popularity, and I flatter myself that we took advantage of it and did Conrad a service. I tried to see Conrad in London a number of times,

* The George H. Doran Company, founded in 1908, was absorbed by Doubleday, Page & Company in 1927 and the firm name was changed to Doubleday, Doran & Company.

but he was so embarrassed and shy that he would not permit it. When *Chance* became a success, however, I insisted to Pinker that I should have an opportunity to talk with the author. I shall never forget the day when Conrad came to lunch with me at Brown's Hotel in London, nervous to the last degree and at first hardly able to talk intelligently. I asked him what work he was doing, and he became interested in telling me about the new book which was on the stocks at that time. He forgot himself, and in fifteen or twenty minutes we were thoroughly at home together, and were intimate friends from then until the date of his death. It was a great satisfaction to think that we were able to earn for him a very substantial amount of money, I should say something over two hundred thousand dollars, so at least he was no longer under the whip of poverty.

In the fall of 1922 we were in London and I said to him, "Mr. Conrad, we have made you many visits, but you have never made us one. Don't you think you should return our calls?"

"When would you like me to call?" he asked.

I said, "The first of May," and the first of May he came.

I cannot possibly describe the pleasure which this visit at Oyster Bay gave us. As a visitor he was both a most delightful person and the greatest nuisance. His personality was charming, but the newspaper reporters who flocked around were tiresome beyond words, and we were deluged with letters, telegrams, and telephone messages.

Our friend Chris[topher] Morley met him at quarantine and helped him through the troublesome time with the reporters, who were so vigorous and so full of questions that he almost collapsed. Chris also wrote innumerable articles about Conrad and was of the utmost assistance in making his visit a success.

Of all the foreign visitors who have made the journey to New York, I think Conrad was perhaps the most successful. This came about through his perfectly simple and open manner. I asked him, for instance, if he was going to lecture, and he replied that the people of the United States had always been very kind to him and he saw no reason why he should lecture them—as a matter of fact, he had come only to visit a friend, not for business. This seemed very striking, and started the Conrad publicity ball going in a way which I thought remarkable and certainly unusual.

He came over to Garden City several times and seemed to feel that he was a part of the organization. He went so far as to try to make a speech to some of the heads of our departments, but practically broke down. A curious thing about Conrad was that, while he wrote the most beautiful English, he spoke it in such a way that it was extremely difficult to understand. For instance, two stenographers tried to take down his speech at Garden City, but they could understand only a few words.

We had many experiences together, and if I should recount them all, it would pad out this volume to unwieldy proportions. One of the most trying things that ever happened to me was his effort to make a speech at the home of Arthur Curtiss James and to read from *Victory*. It was given to me to introduce him to the audience. He was in a state of nervous collapse, and I was not far behind. I remember that I was almost in a trance when I got up to make the introduction, and I was surprised to hear myself say, "This is the first time that Mr. Conrad has ever spoken in public, and please God, if I have anything to do with it, it will be the last."

It was the last. It nearly killed him, because of his extraordinary nervousness.

During his visit to us we took him on a journey to New England, which he enjoyed beyond words. He had never been to the United States before, one must remember, and the experience was unique. He was the sweetest, most delightful man that one would meet in a year's journey; he took his part in the family affairs, and when there was entertaining to be done, he was sure to carry his end of the load.

Eventually we took him home and delivered him to his wife and got a receipt for him. She admitted that he was in better health when he arrived home than when we took him, and it is one of the pleasantest things in my life that we should have been able to be of service to a man of his character and extraordinary charm.

It is also a pleasure to think that we deserve some credit for establishing his reputation in America, where his sales were always much larger than in England. I like to think, too, that American readers appreciated him more than the English ever have, and I think that Conrad felt the same way.

One of the most dramatic things that ever happened was the sale of his manuscripts, most of which had been purchased by an Irishman named John Quinn for fifty dollars apiece or thereabouts. They were sold at auction for one hundred and ten thousand dollars, of which Conrad got, of course, not one cent beyond the price of the original purchases. I tried to get Quinn to divide up with J.C., but without success.

There was one episode in his life which, so far as I know, he kept secret except from me and possibly a few intimate friends—I never heard anyone else speak of it. Several universities in England wished to give him degrees, which he would not accept. He said he was a plain sailorman, and if he accepted degrees, he would more or less cast aspersions on the value of this distinguished honor; and nothing could induce him to change his mind.

When he came to America, Yale University notified him that they would like to confer a degree upon him, and I had the job of getting him out of it, which was not an easy thing to do, as such degrees are not often declined. On our New England visit we stopped overnight at the home of William Lyon Phelps† in New Haven, and both Phelps and Conrad promised that they would go the next morning to see the secretary of the university, thank him for the honor of suggesting a degree, and decline it in a way which would not give offense. When we got fifty miles beyond New Haven on our way east, I asked Conrad how he had gotten along with the secretary of the university. He said he was sorry to say that he had forgotten all about it. Again I had to make up a story the best I could to explain why it was impossible for Mr. Conrad to accept a degree. Of course, having declined several English and Scotch degrees, this made it a trifle easier, but it was rather a delicate business.

In 1924 I received a letter from Conrad saying not to

† Literary critic and Yale professor.

tell anybody, but he had received a communication from the Prime Minister in the shape of a long envelope which looked very official and he was sure he had violated the income tax laws and would probably go to jail. He opened the envelope with trepidation to find that he was to be known thereafter as Sir Joseph Conrad. This honor threw him into a tremor of excitement; he did not want to be known as Sir Joseph Conrad and was absolutely opposed to having a title. Just how he got out of it, I never heard. He told me to keep it to myself, which I did, and I do not believe that many people knew that the honor had been proffered to him, which was perhaps just as well.

My correspondence with Conrad was voluminous and affectionate. It is in the safe, and will be valuable and interesting sometime.‡

‡ Conrad's papers are now at the Yale Library; Mr. Doubleday's personal correspondence is at Princeton.

CHAPTER XVII

GARDEN CITY

[Editor's Note: Effendi wrote, in another manuscript, an essay on attractive places-of-work, from which the next few pages are excerpted. The story of Garden City, page 134, is from the original manuscript of his memoir.]

Brooklyn was my birthplace, and I was ten or twelve years old before I learned to register from "New York."

In our block in South Brooklyn there lived a millionaire. It was evident that he was a millionaire, because he had a most elaborate place, both inside and out. On the outside was a high iron fence which was supposed to keep boys out of his garden. It didn't.

His house was conspicuous in every way; he was proud even of his bronze statues, which he thought distinguished his lawn. Everything was done to make his place look attractive, and when we were invited to his parties we were always duly impressed by the lavish expenditure of money.

I also knew his son, who was as proud of his possessions as was his father. The boy once invited me to the house to see the pictures and objets d'art which were stored within it, including statuettes of plaster manufactured by a commercial artist named Rogers. At the entrance to the house was an old-time servant with powdered hair and knee breeches—the acme of successful living in that community at that time. No expense was spared for anything which would add comfort or luxury to the establishment.

At another time I was invited to the factory where the patent medicine which provided all this luxury was compounded. This was done by hand in the old days and the output was insignificant compared with what is done at the present time; but to me it was an opportunity to see how and where a millionaire made his fortune. The entrance to the factory was an old stairway which I think had not been cleaned for a year. All the processes of making the patent medicine were crude and unscientific. I doubt if a man didn't sometimes get quinine when he was looking for bicarbonate of soda; but though the methods were rough, they answered the purpose of keeping the millionaire in funds.

The millionaire's son was just as proud of the factory as he was of the plaster statuettes in the parlor of his home. One was where he lived and had his being; the other was where he worked and created his wealth. I pondered long and seriously to try to solve the question why he should have such a dirty, unattractive factory where he spent most of his waking hours, and pour out his money so freely in buying things which he thought would ornament his house. For years I thought about my millionaire friend; I was never able to figure out why an attractive factory would not make more money than an unattractive one.

With this background of interest in the commercial value of sunshine and air, I have watched all the experiments which have come within my vision in the hope that I should find someone who believed that there was profit in sunshine and would develop the idea; but I have had little success in finding people who think that their factory can be as attractive as their home.

Henry Ford, that marvel of business genius, realized the value of cleanliness and order, and the factories where he and his son spend their time are as orderly as any home, with the result that they make more money and have more pleasure than anyone else who is trying to do the same thing, in my knowledge.

My millionaire friend has passed away and, I think, his patent medicine with him. There has sprung up during the years that have intervened a desire for attractive, up-to-date, and efficient business offices with better conditions for workers. About the best architecture in this country is found in its present office buildings; a man spends his lifetime in the most attractive offices he can create, with good light, good ventilation, and good sanitary conditions, and takes a well-deserved pride in the change from the sordid, ill-kept offices of the past to the best of modern architecture.

But unfortunately the idea has not yet really spread to factory design, though we know from the few who have tried it that sunshine is capable of distilling profits.

As I look back on it, I must have been an awful bore. I would tell my story about the money value of good surroundings to any victim who fell into my hands. The shortest version, I could give in about five minutes; but I liked to have ten minutes to cover thoroughly all the points. I never succeeded in getting more attention than ten minutes, and there were few people who would listen as much as that.

In the same block with the palace of the millionaire lived an old friend named Charley Barnes. He was a life insurance agent, and the merits of insurance were impressed upon me until I realized I was much more valuable dead than alive. He was an orator and could describe most vividly the happy position in which you would find yourself if you only had thousands of dollars' worth of insurance.

Of course I tried my attractive business scheme on him: so far as I know, I was the only man of our acquaintance who could keep up a long argument with the capacity of Charley Barnes. After years of talk, I induced him to try the experiment of beautifying his office. After he got started he went rather farther than I had recommended.

The Barnes office consisted of one room in a building several scores of years old. Nothing daunted, he started in. First, he cleaned up his place, painting his office a sage green. Then he installed six wire canary bird cages with the accompanying birds intact, some goldfish in a glass globe, put rugs on the floor, and attractive glass shades on his gas fixtures (this was before the days of electricity), and did everything he could to make the room fit for the Sultan of Zanzibar.

The only convert I ever made developed the idea into an income-earning affair beyond anything that I had foreseen. An insurance agent considers half the battle won when he can attract the interest of his prospects. If this is true (and I think it is), Charley's scheme had back of it the basis of a fortune. He would invite a victim to come and see his rugs and curtains and have afternoon tea, and would sometimes get the hapless, helpless guest to bring his wife, who would be greatly benefited by the insurance which would develop provided she only bided her time. When he got his visitors inside the office, little was said about insurance, although the interest of the invited was very much aroused.

He grew rich. But his psychology worked on his system so effectively that he died in one of his own insurance talks, as if to prove a point.

Still my faith was unshaken, and I firmly resolved that if I ever became the controlling factor in a business, I would work out the plan that had been in my mind for years.

However ambitious and energetic I was, everything seemed to break against carrying out the plan. After I left Scribner's and went into partnership with McClure, I had to move into a powerhouse on Lexington Avenue and Twenty-fifth Street to create a publishing business. The surroundings were about as unattractive as one could imagine; but I confess that even a powerhouse was cleaner than any of the offices offered for rent at that time.

On the first of January 1900, we reorganized the publishing business, Sam McClure dropping out and Walter Page taking his place. We moved into a small office on Union Square, and there for the first time I put a few plans in execution. Instead of wooden partitions built by the mile, we worked out offices which were not unattractive —very convenient and comfortable and with good light. Here we enjoyed life for several years until we built our own building on Sixteenth Street. This was colonial in style and had all the conveniences that the law allowed in those early days.

The idea of better and more attractive working conditions was still alive in my brain (in fact, I have never lost sight of it and am still obsessed by the same notion). The result was our move to Garden City and the establishment of the Country Life Press. Much to my surprise, the whole world was not excited on the subject; Country Life Press interested fewer people than I had hoped outside of our own shop. Many people prophesied its failure, but the idea of failure never crossed my mind.

A myth which I think has been exploded is the venerable story that workmen don't care what their surroundings are—if you build a house for them and put in a bathtub, they will fill it with coal, etc. This story has been current for twenty-five years; but I am frank to say that I have been unable to find any lack of appreciation of the things one does to make people at work comfortable and happy.

When we had decided that we were going to move out of town, the big question was where we should move. I remember one of our associates, Houston, had an idea which he persistently pressed upon us all. It made me shiver. He wanted us to buy a lot in the heart of Newark, right next to a railroad track, and move the whole business there. Fortunately for me, nobody agreed with him, and after a while we forgot it.

We were attracted to Long Island particularly by the fact that the Pennsylvania Railroad had just bought the Long Island Railroad and put the tunnels under the river, which seemed to make a place like Garden City more convenient for reaching New York. We began negotiations for a plot in Mineola, and ultimately settled in the place where we now are, Franklin Avenue, Garden City.

Mr. Gage E. Tarbell was the real estate agent through whom we dealt. He was all for getting us to settle in Garden City, but Mr. Evarts, the president of the Garden City Company, was not so enthusiastic, especially as he had a contract with all the homeowners that no manufacturing would ever be permitted in Garden City. I did not see myself how it could be worked out and even a place as beautiful as the planned Country Life Press could be built with this contract in existence. However, this was not my business and Tarbell had to manage it.

When we came to negotiate for buying the property, John Petit, the architect who designed Country Life Press, helped us by making all kinds of fancy sketches, not only of the building, but of imaginary gardens, fountains, etc. These drawings, which were very attractive, we sent one after another to the Garden City Company, and I think they produced an atmosphere which ultimately led to our success in buying a large amount of property for a nominal sum. Almost at the last minute we asked for eighteen acres more on the west side of Franklin Avenue, making about thirty-seven acres in all; and while the going was good, we closed the deal for this large acreage at approximately six hundred dollars an acre plus some advertising— I forget how much, but not anything very severe. Mr. Hubbell, the manager of the Garden City Company, told me privately to get all the acreage that I could at this time, because I would never have another chance. All of which turned out to be true, though I had some difficulty in explaining why we wanted so much land, and the Garden City people insisted on our making an agreement not to build on or to sell any of this property for ten years, which was, of course, satisfactory to us, as we did not wish to go into the real estate business, but to have this fine acreage to make our financial statement more attractive.

We went to the Nassau Bond & Mortgage Company, of Mineola, a local institution of importance, and got them to give us an estimate of the real value of this property. They said it was worth three hundred and five thousand dollars, and we put this in among our assets. As it turned out, this was not necessary, and it would have been much better if we had not made any such valuation, as I think it disturbed our taxes and cost us some money in the way of real estate expense; but at that time we were carrying a big burden of bank debts, and it seemed desirable for us to have all the assets we could muster, or, at all events, we thought it was desirable. I suppose the property is now worth eight thousand to ten thousand dollars an acre, so we did not have such a bad bargain, after all.

We got possession of the property in the spring of 1910, and actually began work, I think, in May of that same year. To the best of my recollection and belief, the whole shop—building and equipment—was completely finished in ninety-three working days. This included the machinery, electrical power, and even curtains for the windows, and, roughly speaking, all our gardens; so that when we moved in on the first of October 1910 our idea was really established and could be witnessed by anybody who had eyes to see.

I remember one thing that helped us in working out the gardens. We had a teamster on the place who had the misfortune to drive his horses into an electric train. This incident was bad for the horses and the owner, but good for us. He came to me in great distress, as it was a very serious loss to him and he could only get paid for his team at the end of a long lawsuit; and a lawsuit against the railroad company was not an attractive thing to begin on or to end on. I suggested that he go to the powers that be of the Long Island Railroad and ask that, instead of paying for the horses, they should let him take the topsoil off the right-of-way between the fence and the rail. There was a huge amount of soil which was of no particular value to the railroad. This he did, and I agreed to buy the topsoil at the cost of hauling with a profit for him. I cannot tell how many hundreds of loads of topsoil we got, but enough to put a couple of feet of good soil on the gravel in the court where the fountains are now, with a plentiful supply of rich earth in the rest of the gardens. I wish we had taken more than we did, but we had in mind the expense, and of course we had greatly overrun our estimate, as happens in all the building operations that I know anything about.

When I look back on this experience, I do think we had our courage with us. We had never printed a book, or made a plate, or created a cloth-bound volume. We had to trust practically to new people to develop the (to us) new art of book making. On October 1, 1910, we changed our address from Sixteenth Street, New York, to Garden City, and moved the machinery that we had for printing the magazines one press a day, keeping the presses running so that we could get out our magazines on time. It was a hectic job but was carried through without much difficulty or anxiety. We were fortunate in having a number of earnest and faithful friends in the printing department, and they helped to teach other people who knew nothing of printing or presses or binding.

I well remember the day that the letters came to Garden City from New York. It seemed an overwhelming task to take care of them, but we did take care of them and things went with extraordinary smoothness as I look back upon the experience. Before the first of November of that same year we were well established and at home in Garden City with an ample force and hundreds of applications for work. So this dreaded operation was completed without much nerve racking; in fact, I do not think any of us worried at any time—we just went along with the job.

In 1910 the art of flying was very young and most of it consisted of hopping three or four feet off the ground, with a jump of a hundred feet or so. There was one dare-devil named Hamilton who flew like a lark, and one day he went clean over the building, very much to the excitement of all concerned. We invited him to luncheon, and he was among the earliest signers of our guest book, in which he wrote:

On August 20, 1910 I had the pleasure of looking down upon the new Doubleday, Page & Company building.
Charles K. Hamilton

I took a trip myself in 1910. It just happened that [my son] Nelson and I were over in the flying field, and I was invited to go in a sort of omnibus which lifted itself from the earth by herculean effort. I thought I would surely fall through the braces which I was permitted to cling to; but I did not and enjoyed the trip very much. I confess that when we got a few hundred feet above the earth and the operator shut off the power, I thought that was the end of me. It was simply that he had turned the plane down to glide to earth; it was like sliding down the side of a cellar door. I have been up since, but I think that this was the most thrilling experience in the air that I have ever had.

I was more concerned in building the Garden City place than any of my partners, as I spent most of my time on the job while the rest of them were making money to pay for it in New York. I demanded of the workmen many things which seemed foolish at the time, but which I think have proved to be for the best. For instance, all the plans contained a very large, high chimney running up perhaps eighty to one hundred feet. I put my foot down on this and said we would not have any such chimney, which would spoil the whole idea. The engineer said it was impossible to get along without it, but I insisted that it should not be built. Fortunately for me, he went to Europe about this time, and Petit also went, so I was boss of the job myself. We had a very good superintendent of works; he was a wise old fellow who knew pretty much everything about building that anybody could know, and I acted on his advice. He told me to build a chimney twice as wide as the one that was to ascend into the air, and put on a forced draft, which we did, carrying the chimney just above the roof line, but out of sight. This was a great relief to me, but when the engineer came back, he said I had ruined the efficiency of the building. I believe it turned out that it cost about ten cents more an hour, or something like that; at all events, it contributed to my happiness not to have this accursed chimney.

The next snag that I struck with the professional engineer was the necessity of a wooden tank on the roof for fire purposes. I insisted upon it that I would not have this, and suggested putting in a pool just west of the building which would hold a hundred thousand gallons of water and be attached to a big pump. This the engineer and most of the people on the job said was a foolish expense, but my old friend the superintendent, whose name I think was Anderson and whose memory shall be ever blessed in my mind, told me that I was a fool not to have what I wanted, and if it cost a few hundred dollars more, I had better borrow it and work it into my plans.

So the pool, which has become one of our most attractive features, was built. I had a picture of a pool at the Villa Falconieri, in Frascati, near Rome, surrounded by cypress trees, and we fairly well reproduced this effect in cedars which we brought from miles around.

There was one funny incident which I never told anybody; I was too much ashamed of myself. The architects drew an elaborate set of plans for certain fancy additions to the building, and I could not get them to give up this idea. In the first place I thought it was unsuitable; in the second place, it was very expensive; and in the third place, it was a time-consuming affair. One night after everybody had gone, I saw these plans and drawings lying on the architect's desk in the shanty which always holds things of this kind; and I took them and buried them under the steps in the front of the building with about fifty good-sized brickbats and rubbish of various kinds on top of them. There they are to this day.

The next morning the fight was resumed, and I brought things to a head by saying, "Well, let's get the plans and look them over and see what we can do."

So there was a wild scurrying for the plans, which could not be found. As the burial had been committed on the original drawings, there were no duplicates; the whole thing had disappeared and everybody was wild with excitement that such a thing could have happened. I trust I was sympathetic. At all events, I said: "This work has got to be done quickly. It will cost us a lot of money and take a lot of time to redraw the plans, and if they are not here, we will go on without them and cut out the fancy work." This the architect could not help, so I was relieved of something that really troubled me.

I must confess that I never enjoyed anything more than the building of this plant. The superintendent, Anderson, was a most delightful character. He worked ostensibly for the builder, but actually he worked for and with me and was full of wise advice. For example, I remember very well that the specifications called for, I think, six or seven inches of concrete on the cellar floor. I said to him, "This seems an awful lot of material to bury in this place. Do you regard it as necessary?"

He said, "You can cut it in half and it will be just as good, if not better."

So we cut it in half, and so far as I know the cellar floor has never risen up to call us cursed.

This was only one of a dozen things that happened. It is a great thing in building to be able to have a direct connection with the builder and cut out the long circuitous relation from builder to architect and from architect to owner. In this case we had an ideal relation which it was possible to work out successfully largely because of the personality of Anderson. I could not begin to tell how much money we saved through his advice as well as courage. He stood the chance of being sacked by his own employer, the builder, but he went on calmly and I hope has grown rich since, as he deserves everything that is coming to him.

We also had an assistant in the way of a clerk of the works representing us, named Jerome. He, too, helped, and the three of us had a grand time. Sam Everitt, Henry Lanier, Russell [Doubleday] and Page were all busy in New York and lost a lot of fun that I acquired. In the middle of the enterprise I had to go to Europe, which took, I think, about a month; but everything went on swimmingly, the pace having been set by our co-operation as already described.

One little thing which is hardly worth telling about but which I happen to think of was the plate in the middle of the front walk to the main entrance. As it happens, the building is set with the four corners of the compass. We figured out how many miles it was to the North Pole, how many miles to the South Pole, how many miles to Australia, etc., and put these distances in a compass-shaped plaque embedded in the bricks. The idea was an incident which amounted to nothing, but many people have stood and studied how far they would have to go to get to the North Pole—which reminds me of Mark Twain's story of standing around, looking for the Langham Hotel, and asking a policeman if he could walk to the Langham and how far it was. The policeman replied, "If you walk in the direction you're facing, it's about twenty-four thousand miles; but if you turn around and walk the other way, it's about one hundred and fifty yards."

When the plans for the Country Life Press had been completed, I asked Mr. Mifflin, of Houghton Mifflin Company, if he would look them over. He said that he would do more than that—he would be glad to come down and see the building as far as it had progressed and study the plans with us.

This he did, and he criticized it as not being large enough. He said, "You are growing at a pace which will soon leave you in a crowded condition, especially your stockroom."

This surprised me, as the place looked truly enormous:

[143]

I wondered if we were ever going to have enough books and machinery and people to make it look inhabited at all.

Mr. Mifflin was right: I do not think it was more than two or three years before we had to put up a new building for storage purposes on the east side of the railroad track. This building was finally extended until it is now about six hundred feet long. More than this, we had to hire miserable shacks in Camp Mills, the government reserve, to store paper boxes and rough material of that sort. We should have done much better if we had carried out Mr. Mifflin's idea, as building was cheap in 1910 compared with anything that has occurred since in the way of building prices.

We have always been delighted to see visitors, even printers who were trying to get some ideas from our practices. I think this is a purely American invention. I remember particularly that Henry Ford in his new book expresses his desire that anyone who may be benefited should come and study his methods in his great shop. We had precisely the same feeling, and one of the men who was most interested was Sir William Berry, the proprietor of Cassell & Company, of London, and other publishing enterprises. He much amused me with a thousand questions. For instance, he said:

"You sell preferred stock to your employees, and have paid for a number of years, I understand, something between eighteen and nineteen per cent for your money, following out the idea of a bonus to those who deserve it. At what rate could you have borrowed the money at the bank?"

"Probably five per cent," I replied, whereupon he inquired:

"Isn't that a terrible extravagance—the difference between five per cent and eighteen or nineteen per cent which
you actually pay?"

I said, "It may be an extravagance, but it seems to me a
fine investment."

He could not see it, but his wife, who sat by, turned to
him and said, "Billy, you are getting some information
which you have never thought of. You had better remember
all this experience."

I was quite flattered by Lady Berry's criticism.

I wanted to study English methods, and asked permission
for John Hessian to go to see the Nelson printing and
binding works. I had considerable difficulty in getting
permission, because they were afraid that he would steal
some ideas; but as we were three thousand miles away,
they finally let John go through the building. I am sorry
to say that I do not think he found anything which would
help us very much, but all over England at that time
every little advantage of the smallest importance was kept
secret, in the hope that it would benefit the owner at the
expense of outside people. I think this is passing away, and
a good job, too.

Speaking of the printing business—I have always been
convinced myself that the reason we have done so well
with Country Life Press is that we have all worked
together to keep it fully employed and to gain everything
possible in the way of efficiency, like strict co-operation in
all the departments. An ordinary printer working for a
customer has to please the customer, who often, if not

always, demands absurdly unreasonable things which he does not expect to pay for and which must come out of the printer. Country Life Press has been assisted by all departments demanding nothing which is not necessary. I think this close co-operation accounts for our unusual profits, and I hope it will continue and grow as the days go by. I hope the same thing, also, for the Windmill Press in Kingswood in connection with the Heinemann business. I am sure we shall achieve the same co-operation there that we have had in Garden City.

When we were young and frisky we used to have all kinds of parties. I remember that on Sixteenth Street we had a housewarming. Each of our magazines had a booth, and each was different. For instance, we had live bees, poultry, and many kinds of country things where *Country Life* was situated. We invited all our friends to tea, and I think had two or three hundred. We kept up our parties for years—with increasing difficulty, because the force grew so large. One of the largest and pleasantest we had was when Mr. Page came home for his vacation in 1916, when we gave a dinner party at the McAlpin Hotel. I think there were more than a thousand. Page told us some confidential stories, and it was a delightful occasion, which I am sure gave him as much pleasure as it did the rest of us.

One of the best of these stories, which has never been printed, could not very well have been printed, partly I think because it contained something in the way of imag-ination on Page's part.

It seems that half a dozen Oxford dons had gone to Constantinople to read some famous manuscript. The war burst right in their faces and the Turks immediately clapped them into jail. It does not take much imagination to realize the miseries of Oxford dons confined in a Turkish jail. They suffered a good deal until they finally were able to communicate with the American ambassador, Henry Morgenthau.

He went to Enver Pasha and tried to touch his heart with the story of the sufferings of these old men. Enver said that they would be released for a payment of about fifty thousand Turkish pounds. Then ensued a long negotiation, and finally Mr. Morgenthau purchased their release for, I think, about ten pounds apiece.

He immediately communicated with Ambassador Page and asked that England should arrange for the repayment of this money and the transfer of the men to an English ship so that they could get home. Page had to take up the matter with Sir Edward Grey, the Minister of Foreign Affairs.

He said, "Sir Edward, are you in want of any Oxford dons this morning?"

Sir Edward replied that he was not inclined to purchase dons—but did Page have some to sell?

Page said yes, he did—six—which the American ambassador owned, having paid for them at the rate of about ten pounds apiece; that he would be glad to turn them over to the English authorities for the same amount, and Sir Edward could, if he chose, repay Mr. Morgenthau.

Sir Edward replied that it was not England's custom to pay tribute; although they sometimes paid expenses; and he handed Mr. Page a check for the amount.

Thus the Oxford dons with their long gray beards intact reached London and home.

After we moved to Garden City we had dancing parties, moving picture parties, and excursions in summer to various places—two or three times up the Hudson River, when we hired our own boat and filled it full of our own staff. Another time we went down to Port Jefferson. I am sure these excursions gave pleasure to everybody, especially as they brought the members of the different departments together. The only difficulty that I can see is that we ought to have a new idea for every party, otherwise they may become a tiresome affair.

Then, too, we had authors' garden parties, one of which is immortalized in a film which Russell had made, showing the author, Ernest Thompson Seton, getting off the train with his manuscript, following it through the works to its ultimate completion, and its shipment out of the south door directly to the railroad train. This film has been shown to millions of people and I think is still traveling around the country.

We sent a positive to England for them to show there. They invited some authors and gave an exhibition of the film at the Hyde Park Hotel. The next day the *Morning Post* had a little article on this moving picture show, and flattered us by saying that Country Life Press in Garden City occupied most of Long Island. The *Morning Post* always was a conservative paper.

We had a plan which we never carried out very far, to get distinguished authors to plant trees as souvenirs of their visits. Such a tree, a Douglas spruce, was planted by John Muir, and a sugar maple (his favorite tree) by John Burroughs. They are standing in the garden today.

On Christmas Day, 1910, Mr. Page had a little Asiatic

flowering crab on his dining table. This he transferred the next spring to the Country Life Press grounds—a very charming memorial. It has grown strong and healthy and is quite a conspicuous little feature.

A few years ago we put up a greenhouse to supply the plant with flowers in the winter; and a laboratory for *Radio Broadcast Magazine.* By the way, the other day in the laboratory near the greenhouse, we received messages from Tahiti at a very low wave length—I think on about the power that it takes to run an ordinary small flashlight.

I remember the beginnings of my interest in radio. Arthur Page gave me a letter to General Squier, who was with Walter Page in England as one of his aides. He showed us what they were doing with radio at that time and let us listen in to communications which were being received at the Navy Station in Washington from England, France, Italy, etc. This stirred my blood, as I thought it was one of the most remarkable experiences I had ever had, and I got a radio set myself as soon as I was able to purchase one. Shortly followed the starting of the magazine, *Radio Broadcast,* which I hope and believe will be a success for many years; at all events, it has got a good start.

CHAPTER XVIII

MAGAZINE VENTURES

The World's Work and *Country Life* were not our only magazine ventures; as a matter of fact, we were eager to extend our list of periodicals, and the first essay was with the *Garden Magazine*. We were a little fearful lest it should interfere with *Country Life,* but it did not seem to, as *Country Life* went on prospering.

We never had such a clear idea for the *Garden Magazine* as for the others, and in all the years that we have been publishing it, it has taken its share of expense, but I do not believe it has made any money. At one time our idea was to make it as cheaply as possible and get out that way; but I am thankful to say that we overcame this notion, and it is today a handsome magazine, just beginning, I think, on a great future. Its advertising is several times as great as it was; its contents are much improved; its general appearance is attractive; and I think we are off on a fine start with a property which will be increasingly valuable.

Then we started another magazine called *Farming,* which was a dead failure. Garden City did not offer a suitable atmosphere, and after running it a few months we killed it.

Later on we started a health magazine, with the same experience. It was designed to cover the field of physical culture, which was at that time having a great vogue; but we did not have the spirit to make it popular with all kinds of nude figures; we tried to make it respectable and only succeeded in making it dull. After a few months we chopped its head off and accepted, I think, a considerable loss.

Also there came to us *Short Stories,* which is described in the following chapter, and this was followed by two other fiction magazines, the *Frontier* and *West.* Neither of the last two has succeeded as yet, but I feel that they will succeed in the near future. Another successful venture in the periodical field was *Le Petit Journal,* a little paper for people who wish to carry on their work in French; and *El Eco* does the same thing in Spanish. Both of these periodicals are very successful and making good profits.

Still another of our magazines is the *Educational Review,* edited by William McAndrew, of Chicago. This is, I think, one of the livest periodicals we have in the place; it ought to be as good as the *American Mercury* and sell as many copies; but there seems to be no way of working this out, as McAndrew is superintendent of schools in Chicago, and can only do his end of the magazine job with his left hand.

We once purchased an interest in a magazine called *Dress,* and proved to our satisfaction that we did not know anything about fashions or dress, nor did we have the ability to run a periodical of this sort. Houston sold it eventually to Condé Nast for a huge price, because, as I remember, Nast was afraid that Hearst was going to buy it and start up an active competition with *Vogue*. As a matter of fact, we had had no communication with Hearst, and never at any time expected to sell it to him. I have forgotten how much money this sale netted us, but we even had a share in the profits when it became profitable, which it did after Nast had spent four hundred thousand dollars. He turned it into a magazine called *Vanity Fair*.

I hope these lessons in trying to make magazines on subjects with which we were not familiar and in which we were not really interested will sink in and that we will not do anything foolish hereafter—a vain hope, as everybody has to do something foolish to keep within the game. On the whole, we have pulled off some pretty good magazines, and there is no reason to complain.

CHAPTER XIX

THE TALE OF
A SUCCESSFUL FAILURE

WE HAD a rotary press which was used for *The World's Work* and was not occupied all the time. Mr. Etherington was supplying paper for a magazine entitled *Short Stories,* and he had loaned the proprietor some eight or ten thousand dollars which the owner could not pay. He asked me if we could take it over and print it, and keep an eye on the editorial policy.

This we were only too glad to do, but the first thing we knew the magazine owed us eight or ten thousand dollars for printing, with no good prospect of its being paid. This was a situation that looked almost hopeless, but I found out that the profit on the printing would almost equal our losses, so we kept on.

Gradually, month by month, and year by year—for it took several years—short story magazines came into popularity, and the first thing we knew the sale had gone up to forty or fifty thousand. We then had the courage to go in and buy literary material of a popular and more expensive

type; and, to make a long story short, we made so good
a magazine, which appealed to so large a class of buyers,
that eventually we got the circulation up to two hundred
and fifty thousand twice a month, and as all the world
knows, it has been one of the most profitable things we
have ever owned.

The title, I thought, was very valuable, as a man would
go to the newsstand and say he wanted short stories,
meaning a magazine of short stories, and he always got
the one with the big moon on it, much to our advantage.

There was still quite a lot of stock of the magazine in
the hands of Mr. Harold Godwin, who had advanced
the proprietor some money. Mr. Etherington bought this
stock and I think was really involved to the tune of
something like thirty thousand dollars. He made an offer
to us that if we would pay back to him what he had
invested he would turn over this stock to us and we
would own the magazine completely. As it became increasingly profitable, this was not a difficult thing to do,
and it was not many years before the right and title to the
whole property rested in the hands of Doubleday, Page &
Company. It has been one of our most fortunate ventures.

For some reason, we thought that it would sell also in
England. We took the old numbers and sent them abroad,
in the hope that we would get at least a few cents a
copy. This was the beginning of an English edition, printed
in England but using the American plates. It has been
a success, and I think the latest statement of circulation
shows that they are printing something like forty thousand
copies a month and making a handsome profit.

Later on we sent *West,* another fiction magazine, over

to England, and at the present writing it looks as though it would be equally successful. All of which is astonishing to me, because both of these magazines are most strikingly American in every sense of the word. Many of the phrases used must be entirely unintelligible to the English readers; but somehow they like it, and we are very glad that they do.

Here is another experience which I have no possible way of explaining.

CHAPTER XX

THE STORY OF
THE JUNGLE

I AM not very good at remembering dates, and do not
pretend that all these dates are correct, but we had been
in business, I think, about five years, when I was told by
the advertising department of *The World's Work* that
Armour & Company, the meat packers, of Chicago, had
withdrawn their advertising, notwithstanding that they had
a contract, having given as a reason that we had a manuscript in the place which we were considering, and they
would not continue their advertising until they were assured that the manuscript was rejected. To be held up in
this way naturally made us angry, and while nobody had
paid any particular attention to the manuscript, we hunted
it up and found that it was called *The Jungle,* by Upton
Sinclair.

He was a wild individual, and none of us really wanted
to have anything to do with him; but that a Chicago
butcher should tell us how to run our editorial department we could not stand for. We told the Armour people
that they could withdraw their advertising if they wanted

to, and we would publish the book or not, as we thought best.

At that time we had not the slightest idea that the book would be suitable for publication; but we found on examination that it was a vividly written exposure of terrible things that were going on in the stockyards of Chicago. We did not at first believe the story told in the book, but a careful investigation provided proof that the tale was not overwrought and was essentially true. Under these circumstances, it seemed to us that it was our duty to publish the book. It was a disagreeable job, a disagreeable atmosphere, and a disagreeable incident which we had to accept to appease our own consciences.

We notified Armour & Company that we were going to publish the book, and they replied that they would at once institute a suit for libel for half a million dollars, to which we replied that if they could find half a million dollars around the building and could beat us in a suit they would be welcome to it. The suit never materialized.

We set up and published the book and it attracted very little attention. But the author, Upton Sinclair, sent a copy to President [Theodore] Roosevelt, who wrote us a strong letter asking why we should publish such an obnoxious book as *The Jungle*. We replied that we thought it was our duty—it was not a matter of pleasure or profit—that we had investigated the whole subject and believed that the book in all essential particulars was accurate. I remember he sent for me and told me to bring along my evidence. We had dispatched a young man who was also a lawyer of some ability to make an investigation when we first examined the manuscript. He secured plenty of evidence that bad meat was canned and sold, and had many experiences which are too disagreeable to relate here now that these conditions have long since passed away. All these things were turned over to the President, who instituted an investigation through the Department of Agriculture, the result of which was that the head of the Department reported that the charges were untrue and the stockyards were as pure as the driven snow.

We found that the Armour people had simply bribed the investigators and got a clean bill of health at an extraordinarily small expense.

This report put us in a rather trying position, and the President asked me what we proposed to do about it. I told him that his investigators had simply been dishonest, and finally convinced him that they had not reported on the facts correctly, having, as a matter of fact, been bribed. We found that the vote of one of them had been purchased for one hundred and twenty-five dollars. It is extraordinary to think what the packers were able to do at that time, and for a small amount of money.

The President got very angry about the whole thing. He was convinced that the investigation had been a farce, and he had the evidence brought back and turned over to the Bureau of Commerce and Labor, with another committee to investigate.

Meanwhile, the sales of the book went on in a small way, many people thinking that it was a remarkable publication, and many others, including myself, that it was disgusting. Much to our relief, the second investigation committee reported that the book was essentially true, and they supplied evidence to show that the most horrible things were done regularly in the packing business and concealed with considerable ingenuity. The report of the Commerce and Labor committee the President gave out to the newspapers, and it made a tremendous sensation. The sale of the book immediately moved by leaps and bounds, and there was high excitement because no one knew whether canned meat was good or bad. So far as the packers went, they suffered severely, and under the direction of the government reformed their practices and I presume have lived a godly life since.

But they did not give up easily. One day a man came into my office with a letter of introduction from Frank Seaman, and said that he was Mr. Armour's personal attorney, that Mr. Armour's private car was at the Grand Central Station, and if I would take it and go out to see him, they would give us a three-page contract for each of our magazines and resume friendly relations with us. Of all the unbounded cheek that I ever heard of, this transcended everything, and I immediately went into a fury. I had just received from Lord Northcliffe, an old friend of mine, a cable dispatch asking for permission to reprint *The Jungle* in England and various other places in Europe. We had decided in thinking it over that we had had about all the *Jungle*-bad meat business that we could stand, and we did not care to wash our dirty linen in all the capitals of Europe. But this chap made me so angry, particularly when he offered me some canned meat, that I showed him this telegram and told him we would give permission to have the book reprinted in Europe. He did not seem to understand why I was so angry. Of all the moral degenerates that I ever saw, he was the worst.

Having declined the invitation to go and visit Mr. Armour in his private car—as I had told his messenger, I was not accustomed to traveling in private cars and did not want to establish an expensive habit—and having given permission to Northcliffe to use the material, we awaited results. It was published serially in the London *Despatch* and within a couple of weeks all England was ringing with the exposure of the packing of rotten meat. I am told that it practically ruined the Armour business in Europe.

I felt myself humiliated that I should have been offered a bribe of three pages of advertising for violating my conscience. I must confess that we were all terribly stirred up at the time. Meanwhile, the book kept on selling, and I believe it sells some to this day.

I have often wondered what would have happened if anybody but Theodore Roosevelt had been President when this incident came up. He told me that Mr. Armour called on him to try to mitigate the punishment which the public was bound to give him. I am not sure that the President saw either Armour or his representative; he told me that he would not see them without at least two witnesses being present.

This was one of many experiences I had with Theodore Roosevelt, and his vigor and effectiveness were truly extraordinary. I do not suppose one in a hundred in his position would have gone back on the report of his own Department of Agriculture. Whatever became of the dishonest inspectors I never knew, but I hope they got what was coming to them.

Thus endeth a very smelly incident.

CHAPTER XXI

THEODORE ROOSEVELT

ONE MORE Roosevelt story. I do not recall that anybody has written anything in the line of reminiscences which does not include a story of Theodore Roosevelt. I had decided that this private volume should be different from all other books in this respect, but I yield to the convention.

I knew Colonel Roosevelt very well, as everybody from one end of Long Island to the other did. He gave me his private telephone number so that I could talk with him at any time, and we had many experiences together. He was good enough to lay the cornerstone of the Country Life Press in 1910, and I think always felt a kindly interest in our concerns.

One day I was summoned to luncheon with him at Oyster Bay. I did not want to go. That morning a bee had stung me in my throat, which nearly suffocated me when the sting became swollen, and gave me a ridiculous appearance and a curious voice as well. Nellie thought that I ought to go, so we did.

When we arrived at Sagamore Hill the President was in rough clothes chopping down a tree. There were four or five other guests—the Indian Commissioner, I remember, among others, who, the President told me privately, was a narrow-minded bigot. The luncheon was very amusing and in every aspect highly original, the President carrying the whole thing in his hand. When we were leaving he said to me:

"I understand you are going to Europe."

I said that I was.

He said, "Will you see Kipling?"

I replied that I would, and he said: "Give him my warmest regards and tell him I regret that I have not written to him lately, but that the American people don't owe me a thing—I am having a bully time."

I gave this message to Kipling and he asked me to take back a message in reply. He said: "I was in the tap room of the hotel at Capetown, with Dr. Jameson of Jameson's raid, when a boy brought in the newspaper containing Roosevelt's message about the Panama Canal. Jameson looked it over and handed the paper to me and said, 'The President's message makes me feel like thirty cents as a raider.' Tell this to the President when you go back," Kipling said.

I did not much care to do this and made up my mind that I would never mention the subject. As it happened, a short time after I returned I was one of a committee to ask Roosevelt to make a speech at a publishers' dinner. There were a number of us, and as we filed through his office I kept quiet. Just as I was going out, I heard him say:

"Doubleday, come back here. I want to speak to you." And after the other people had left, he asked, "Did you see Kipling?"

I said that I did.

"How is he?" he asked.

"Well," I replied.

"Did he send me any message?" he inquired.

I hesitated and was lost. Finally I said, "Mr. President, he did mention something, but it was not very important and perhaps I had better not attempt to repeat it, as I may not trust my memory."

He said: "The authority is not given you to decide that question. When you are given a message, it is up to you to give it. What did he say?"

I told him about Dr. Jameson's remark, and rather to my surprise he was quite upset about it and made a long statement justifying his treatment of the Panama President, whoever he was, with whom he made the Panama deal. He sat down at once and wrote Kipling a long letter with his own hand, explaining that South American presidents, if they were put in a box like monkeys, and carted over the mountains and thrown into the sea, would be, he thought, well treated.

The next time I went to see Kipling he told me of the receipt of this letter. After he had looked at it, he went with Carrie into the drawing room and read it line by line and page by page, burning the sheets as fast as they left his hands.

CHAPTER XXII

WRITING
MR. ROCKEFELLER'S
AUTOBIOGRAPHY

A cousin of mine, Julia Doubleday, married one of Mr. Rockefeller's most important secretaries, Starr Murphy. I conceived the idea that Mr. Rockefeller's autobiography would be very interesting, but he was a shy bird, never appeared in the newspapers if he could avoid it, and covered himself with a fog of obscurity which few people were able to penetrate. However, I thought that I would take a chance and talk the matter over with Starr Murphy, who had as much influence with him, I think, as did anyone in his employ.

Much to my surprise, Mr. Murphy did not seem to think the scheme impossible—another example of an experience I have had a hundred times: that plans called impossible, when they are once properly approached, often prove to be not impossible or even very difficult.

To make a fairly long story fairly short, I found that Mr.

Rockefeller was playing golf at the Bon Air, in Augusta. Mr. Murphy would not give me a letter of introduction, but he said that he would write to Mr. Rockefeller, and if Mr. Rockefeller was interested to meet me, he would hunt me up. So it fell out one day that the great oil king took notice of the insignificant publisher and invited me to play golf with him

Rockefeller's golf was the exact reverse of Mr. Carnegie's golf. Carnegie could not stand being beaten and would take the utmost liberties with the score. Rockefeller was strictness itself in counting every stroke. I remember that one tee at Augusta faced a little swamp. If Rockefeller had the misfortune to drive into this morass, he would stop and put on a pair of rubbers, go into the mud, and hammer at his ball, accounting for every stroke. He would keep his score with the utmost care and mark his improvements day by day. Considering everything, he played a remarkable game, and always in strict conformity to the rules.

I could not help but notice that he kept his eye on me when l was not looking; I presume he was sizing me up. I said nothing about his memoirs, hoping against hope that he would introduce the subject himself. One day after eighteen holes he asked me to sit with him a few minutes on the piazza of the hotel. He said:

"I am inclined to ask you to do me a favor, but I fear it might be too much of a task."

I asked him what it was, and tried to indicate that it would be a pleasure to me.

He said: "I would like to tell you the complete story of my life, which I have never told to anybody as yet, not even my own son. In this way I would bring back into my memory things that might escape me, and which are of importance—some of them of public importance. But I would only be willing to ask you to listen with the distinct agreement that if you are bored you will tell me frankly and we will end the sessions."

I told him that I would take a chance on being bored, and if the worst came to the worst, I would stop him in his narrative.

So for two or three weeks every day we sat on the piazza and he told me of all the things that had happened to him since he was a small boy. It was really a tale of thrilling interest, told with a dramatic fervor which kept my attention from the start. Some of these things, of course, were never printed. At that time I think he had no idea of ever printing any of the material; he simply wanted to make a record of it. I feared that the revelations were so intimate that I would never even have the cheek to ask him to give them expression in ink and paper.

One particular story, which will never be printed, he related so cleverly that it gave me a real thrill. He was telling me of the panic of 1907 or 1908 when Mr. Morgan assumed the generalship of the financial world which Wall Street was supposed to give in a panic situation. I think Mr. Rockefeller never greatly admired Mr. Morgan, for the reason, so far as I can see, that Mr. Morgan tried to dominate him and get him to do things which Mr. Rockefeller did not care to do.

I have forgotten just how the subject came up, but Mr. H. H. Rogers, when the panic storm burst, found himself in a bad position with the Virginia Railway, which he owned by himself, I believe, with obligations for a large sum of money when money could not be bought for love nor money. Mr. Rogers finally turned to his old partner, Mr. Rockefeller, and went to his house one afternoon, feeling that he had come to the end of his tether, and unless money could be raised instantly, all his plans and prospects would go up in the air.

Mr. Rockefeller said that, as Mr. Rogers came into the room, he saw that he was trembling with the greatest excitement. He tried to calm him and to be reassuring. Mr. Rogers burst out finally and said that he was ruined—that unless he could have a very large sum immediately, he was beyond help financially.

Mr. Rockefeller moved forward and put his hand on Mr. Rogers's knee and said: "Before you leave this room, you will be in entire mental comfort."

Mr. Rogers was so affected that he almost collapsed. Suddenly he woke up again to his position and said: "What are you going to charge me for it?"

Mr. Rockefeller replied: "This is a matter of friendship, not of money. You will pay not a penny of interest or commission." Then he went to his safe, which he had in his library, and produced securities sufficient to answer Mr. Rogers's requirements and the day was saved.

But to get back to the Rockefeller autobiography. This tale of Mr. Rockefeller's life lasted, I think, for at least two weeks, and when I went home I had the story pretty clearly in my brain, but not a note of any kind. Greatly to my delight, Mr. John D. Rockefeller, Jr., sought me out and said that his father had told him that he had narrated his life story to me. His son was anxious to have me write it out as well as I could remember it and give it to him, as he said it came nearer to a record than anything else that the family had; and as his father was the most abused man in the United States at that time, he and his sisters were eager to have any record which would be of value to them.

I explained that I had made no notes, and I did not know if I could reproduce the conversation with any success, but I would try. I sat down for three or four days and cudgeled my brains to write out this story. I think it amounted to about forty thousand words, and when I finished I gave the record to John D., Jr., for what it was worth. He was very grateful, and asked me if I would go over the material with his father, and correct and amplify the story as I had set it down. This I agreed to do, and I had long sessions with Mr. Rockefeller, reading and re-reading the whole story over and over again, chapter by chapter. I never met a man who was so particular to get things right in detail; sometimes he would make me read certain passages four or five times, and when I showed that I was rather tired of it, he would say, "We will get this right, then we need never think of it again."

When we got the manuscript done, I asked Mr. John D., Jr., if we could publish it in *The World's Work*. He gave me his cordial permission, after consulting with the old man. When we talked about printing it in the magazine, Mr. Rockefeller asked: "How much do you think these articles are worth to you?" and I said, "As I have done an awful lot of work on them, I think perhaps five hundred dollars apiece would be a fair price." He said that if that was satisfactory to me it would be to him, and he actually took the money, five hundred dollars for each article. I tried to get it away from him to give to a blind friend who needed about this sum, but although he gave me some money for my friend, he still retained the major part of it.

I have never been able to understand why this book, which we published under the title, *Random Reminiscences of Men and Events,* by John D. Rockefeller, did not sell. There are two chapters, "The Difficult Art of Making" and "The Difficult Art of Giving," which I think are classics; and coming from the richest man in the world, as he probably was then, they assume an importance which for some reason has never been appreciated.

The success of the articles in the magazine was most complete. They raised the circulation and caused everybody to say that we had sold out to the Standard Oil Company. One incident disabused the public of that idea. While the articles were being published, the Standard Oil Company fell into disrepute, having been proved to have bought the influence of Senator [Joseph B.] Foraker. Mr. Page thought that it was our duty to comment on this subject most severely, condemning the Standard Oil root and branch. I agreed with him, but I told him that I thought we ought to tell Mr. Rockefeller, which I did. Much to my surprise, Mr. Rockefeller said: "If you did not express your opinion honestly, I should think that you were dishonest yourself"; so, while Mr. Rockefeller was still contributing to *The World's Work,* we attacked the Standard Oil Company in the editorial section as only Mr. Page's trenchant pen could do.

Later on Mr. Rockefeller was brought into court to testify about the Standard Oil Company as a trust, and he put in as his evidence the complete contents of this book, and said that he was willing to swear by that and make it his statement of the case.

The book is forgotten, and the whole incident fades away, but to me it was a dramatic experience.

There are two notes which I should like to add to this incident. Not to make the record too long, I may say that the Standard Oil Company did have certain evidence which was not very creditable to Miss Ida M. Tarbell. When Mr. Rockefeller was asked if he wished us to use this in his autobiography, he said on no account; that he would not under any consideration cause any human being the suffering that he had gone through. So the matter was dropped.

Another story revealed the magnitude of Mr. Rockefeller's fortune and how little a million dollars, more or less, mattered. Among his financial adventures was the purchase of the Mesaba Ore mines in the Northwest. He made a huge investment, and at one time it looked as if it was going to be an entire loss. There was much controversy concerning this incident, and many people condemned Mr. Rockefeller, I always thought without reason; but in the end he made a great deal of money. One day I asked him how much he thought he had cleared up on that Mesaba deal. He said he thought about forty million dollars, but that Mr. Gates, his financial secretary, could tell me more exactly.

Gates was a strange individual; he had been a Baptist minister, and was about as shrewd as a man could be. Mr. Rockefeller had appointed him as one of his financial secretaries, mixing in finance, religion, moral practices of various kinds, and creating a situation rather different from anything I ever heard of. I went to Mr. Gates, who knew all the details of Mr. Rockefeller's finances, and told him that Mr. Rockefeller had told me that he thought he had made about forty millions on the ore deal. He said: "Little he knows about it; he made seventy-eight million."

One of the cleverest things that I ever knew John D. to do was in connection with buying some boats which he used to carry his ore across Lake Superior. He wanted to buy six large vessels which were very expensive, and he found out that his chief competitor, Mr. Mather, wanted to buy six also, and they were about to go into the market to give orders for twelve boats.

John D. knew that this would immediately raise the price, and as there were only twelve builders on the lake, he would have to pay through the nose. So he went to Mather and said, "Instead of both of us losing a lot of money, why shouldn't we save a lot of expense? I am willing to put the matter in your hands to do as you think best, but I should like to have you buy me six boats at the same time that you buy yours, and I would suggest that you send out bids for a single boat to each of the ship-builders who could possibly build these vessels. Then I would have them come to your office all at one time, and take them separately, one by one, study the bid and accept it, and then dismiss the builder through another office, so that he would not get back to where the rest of the builders were waiting with their bids."

This Mr. Mather did. He collected the twelve ship-builders and herded them in the office; called them in one at a time; accepted the bid, whatever it was; and dismissed each builder through another office so that he would not get back to his companions.

Apparently the plan worked perfectly, and the men who found themselves each possessed of a contract were indeed surprised. I thought it was an example of John D.'s shrewdness. If he did this in all his transactions, as I suppose he did, it accounts for some of the wealth that he accumulated so rapidly.

CHAPTER XXIII

NEGOTIATIONS
FOR *LIFE*

IF I had a little more assurance, I would write a whole chapter on how to treat a bank. It seems to me that in the publishing business banking associations have usually been weak and ill managed. I had the great good fortune to have the advice of two men who had very broad ideas on banking: Andrew Carnegie and John D. Rockefeller, and I flatter myself that I got much from their conversations.

It is customary to fail to realize the banker's side of any of these questions, particularly those involving loans; and most people do the foolish act of waiting until they need money before they try to borrow it. I was too cautious for this, and we always prepared for our needs long before we were up against it. I remember one time I feared that the Chemical Bank might criticize the size of our loan, and I went to the president and told him that we could use one hundred and fifty thousand dollars if we could get it at the right rate, emphasizing the necessity of borrowing at a low interest when, as a matter of fact, I was afraid he would not lend me the money at all. I always thought that I got this money without real difficulty because I approached the subject from that end.

The most interesting banking incident of my career was, I think, quite remarkable and worth setting down here, especially as it casts as much credit upon Mr. Everitt as it does on the rest of us.

Along about 1919 I was approached by Charles Holt, of Henry Holt & Company, and asked to consider the purchase of *Life,* the humorous weekly. John Ames Mitchell, the editor and inspiration of the paper, had died, and in settling the estate it seemed necessary to sell the periodical.

There were many interviews and there were two possible purchasers: the other stockholders and ourselves. We regarded the magazine as worth more money than did, I think, the people who hoped to acquire it, Charles Dana Gibson in particular. I remember we were willing to pay nine hundred dollars a share, and they wanted to buy it for something like seven hundred dollars. I was going South and left the matter in charge of Mr. Everitt; but before going I went to see Mr. Twitchell, the president of the Chemical Bank, to arrange for a loan of nearly a million dollars which we might need at any minute if the negotiations came to a head and the matter had to be closed up.

Mr. Twitchell, who always seemed to me a most conservative and gentle sort of person, told me that they would be willing to advance the money at any time that I needed it, and I left for the South with the understanding on the part of Mr. Holt and the *Life* executors that nothing would be done until I came back, as there were many adjustments to be made.

That winter we spent a couple of months at Winter Park, Florida. There was a pool nearby into which I was very fond of diving; not wisely but too deep. In my exuberance one day I dove under a big ledge of rock and came up on my shoulder, and broke my collarbone. This put me on the mourners' bench for three weeks, tied up in a very uncomfortable way; and, as so often happens in such cases, the negotiations for *Life* were resumed while I was so far from home and in such a crippled condition.

Mr. Everitt carried on for Doubleday, Page & Company until the situation reached the critical stage and it occurred to him that he might need anything up to a million dollars to make good an offer for the property. Being a wise man, he went to see the Chemical Bank people to inquire of the president, Mr. Twitchell, if he could have the money as arranged with me. He was somewhat alarmed to find that Mr. Twitchell had gone to Florida on a vacation and could not be communicated with at the moment. He talked the subject over with Mr. Halpin, the chief cashier, who said that no doubt Mr. Twitchell had made a memorandum of this, as he did of all such promises. He went through his papers but found no mention of our conversation or agreement. This, he said, was not surprising, because it was so confidential that Mr. Twitchell had probably decided not to make any written record of our talk, but he added: "If you say Mr. Doubleday said that Mr. Twitchell said that you could have a loan of a million dollars for this purpose, I stand ready to provide the money."

I think this was a significant thing. There was not a scrap

of writing anywhere, and that they should take Mr. Everitt's word as to what I said and what Mr. Twitchell said seemed to me to be a compliment to both Everitt and myself.

The deal fell through and Gibson bought the property, I thought for much less than it was worth; and from that day to this, in my judgment, this old and extraordinarily brilliant weekly has steadily decreased in circulation and interest. My own plan was to carry it on exactly as Mitchell did, with the distinct understanding that, if Mitchell did it before, we could do it again. It might have been a great risk, but I feel that we should have made a success of it. Perhaps not, however, and we may be better off without it; at all events, we have our hands fairly full so that time need not hang over us like a cloud.

CHAPTER XXIV

DOUBLEDAY, PAGE
BOOK SHOP COMPANY

IN 1910, when we moved from New York to Garden City, everybody told me that we should never be heard of again; that we would be lost in the wilds of Long Island and no one would even think about us. This got on my nerves after a while, and I almost thought there might be something in it. As a matter of fact, when I told anybody that we were going to move to Garden City, they would immediately say, "Remember, McClure failed at Long Island City; Walker failed at Tarrytown; Munsey failed at New London."*

Finally, this remark so wearied me that I printed a little card as follows:

We have NOT forgotten
McClure in Long Island City
J. Brisben Walker, Tarrytown
F. A. Munsey, New London

* John Brisben Walker, publisher of *Cosmopolitan,* and Frank A.. Munsey, publisher of magazines and newspapers.

So when anybody would begin by saying "Remember . . ."
I would immediately pull out one of these cards and hand
it to him. The invariable reply was: "How did you know I
was going to mention these men?" I said I had learned
after the first five hundred experiences what was apt to
follow in any conversation about Garden City.

But this was not what I started to tell. As everybody was
so sure that we were going to be forgotten, we thought
perhaps it would be worth while to have a foothold in New
York where we might at least display our name. The Pennsylvania Station at Thirty-third Street and Seventh Avenue was just being completed. There were stores in the
arcade, and one of these we rented for a retail bookshop,
as we thought it would be a good thing for people who
lived on Long Island or visited on Long Island to see our
name displayed as prominently as we could get it, and this
seemed to be a good place. This little shop has been there
for sixteen years. I think it has made during this long term
something like a hundred thousand dollars, and has been a
fine place to distribute our own publications direct to our
customers.

The Pennsylvania bookshop did so well that we made
an arrangement with Lord & Taylor to open a shop in their
store at Thirty-eighth Street and Fifth Avenue, and this
did well, too, and still does well. So we gradually increased
the shops until we have, I think, about fifteen.† Notwithstanding the capital requirements, I believe they have made
enough to pay all our capital charges, and the investment

† There are now, in the 1970s, over thirty Doubleday Book Shops
across the country, selling the books of all publishers.

now is small, profits are fairly satisfactory, and the volume of business is approaching a million dollars a year.

Of course, one of the most valuable features is the use of these shops as a barometer to tell what books are selling, what type of books interest people, and what the tendencies are. I believe that the development of the shops might go too far. If we gave the impression that we controlled too much, it would injure our business with the booksellers and perhaps with the public and authors. It is all a very delicate question to discuss and the situation is constantly changing, so there is no use talking about it here.

We have, I think, learned to sell our own books in these shops in competition with the books of other publishers quite successfully. I think that forty per cent of our sales are made up of Doubleday, Page & Company books. Of course it is a little difficult to push our books hard enough and at the same time not displease customers by pressing our wares too strongly. I do not know that we get as much as we should in the way of information from these shops, especially those far away from New York, but we certainly do get much material that is useful, and having a man like [Cedric] Crowell, the manager, attend our weekly book meeting is very valuable and will be increasingly so.

CHAPTER XXV

NELSON DOUBLEDAY, INCORPORATED AND UNINCORPORATED

THIRTY-SEVEN years ago I had the great pleasure of making the acquaintance of one Nelson Doubleday, known later as Nelson Doubleday, Inc. But at that time he had not thought of incorporating.

Later, when he was a boy of about fifteen, he picked up on a visit in Rhode Island a microbe which gave him typhoid, and he was ill more or less for the next five years, which entirely upset all the plans of his parents and made conditions unusually hard. Time hung rather heavily on his hands; he was not well enough to go to work, or to play hard, or to do most of the things that boys enjoy. I suggested to him that he should start a mail-order business, and agreed to put up five hundred dollars capital for this purpose. The idea, I am glad to say, appealed to him, and he hired for about two dollars a month a little shack back of a liquor saloon in Locust Valley.

His circulars soon came to be very original and entirely

unusual and rather daring. His first effort, involving a thousand or two communications to hoped-for book buyers, was entirely unsuccessful. He went to the post office day after day hoping to receive some mail, only to be told that there was nothing in his box. I remember that he found a list of women in New Jersey who owned their own homes, a list which he thought surely would yield orders for Booth Tarkington's books; but these women did not want the books and things were at a low tide.

So he started to change his form of circular. The first one that I remember had printed on the rear flap in imitation handwriting:

> Read the enclosed circular very carefully for two reasons: first, it will be good for you; second, it will be good for me.

I think this particular circular probably started the ball rolling; at all events, business soon began to develop.

Perhaps the most striking letter that he wrote surprised me more than most people. A man said to me one day: "Are you any relation to Nelson Doubleday?"

I admitted that I was by marriage.

"I had a circular letter from him the other day," he said, "in which your name was mentioned."

I begged him to let me see it, and as I remember it, it read somewhat as follows:

Dear Sir:

I was talking with my old friend, Mr. Frank Nelson Doubleday, President of Doubleday, Page & Company, Garden City, Long Island . . . [about such and such a book, and he said such and such things—].

[181]

I asked Nelson why he should bring my name into his circular schemes, to which he replied: "I knew that nobody ever heard of me, but I thought by some chance they might have heard of you."

A particularly original plan of his started about that time. This was the invention of the deferred magazine subscription; that is, he would supply at half price, a month or six weeks after the date of publication, magazines taken from the returns from the News Company. This he developed into a very large list. I think he sold a hundred thousand people or more.

Another advertisement of that time described his office, giving the cost of rent, light, and assistance at a very few dollars a week, and making the appeal to the subscriber that he could thus afford to sell books at prices very much in favor of the customer.

One day I received a note from him in which he enclosed a check for five hundred dollars and said that he was very glad to return this money, which had been so useful and had given him an occupation as well as an income.

These were the beginnings of Nelson Doubleday, Inc., which developed the sale of perhaps a million copies of *Etiquette* and a million dollars' worth of Pocket University and other things too numerous to mention.

When Nelson was about seven or eight years old, Mr. Kipling was writing a series of *Just So Stories*—"How the Elephant Got His Trunk," "How the Leopard Got His Spots," etc. These tales were published in *St. Nicholas* and were vastly interesting to Nelson.

He conceived the idea that if Mr. Kipling would write some more animal stories, the titles of which he suggested, they might be made into a book, and asked if I would mind his writing to Mr. Kipling on the subject.

I said no, whereupon he inquired if I would lend him a five-cent stamp, which he promised to repay, and wrote a long letter in his own fist, addressed to "Rudyard Kipling, Rotting Dean," giving a list of suggestions for new stories about different animals, and adding that if he wrote these stories and they were any good, his father, he was sure, would get them put in book form and give him (Nelson) a royalty of a cent a copy.

The *Just So Stories* finally came out, and Nelson applied for a contract for his cent-a-copy share. This has gone on for twenty or more years, and how much he has received I have no idea, but it must be certainly several thousand dollars. So we shall have to give Nelson credit for having publishing ideas in very early youth.

My partnership with him has been a source of the greatest pleasure and thankfulness. He might reasonably have thought that I was a back number during all these experiences; but if he did, he concealed it in a way which deeply touches me.

CHAPTER XXVI

THE FRENCH BINDERS

SOME ten or twelve years ago Walter Gilliss of blessed memory, who acted as our adviser on typographical matters and stimulated us to produce better and more attractive typesetting, told me of three binders who had been brought over here by Robert Hoe to establish the Club Bindery in connection with the Grolier Club in New York. Slowly but steadily the Club lost interest in these binders, who did very beautiful work at very high prices and did not make expenses; and in the end the association between the binders and the Club Bindery was dropped.

These three men, whose names were Leon Maillard, Henry Hardi, and Gustav Pilon, moved out to Cleveland, in the hope of finding a market there for their great skill. They had all sorts of misfortunes, and when Gilliss first told me of them they were binding magazines for two or three dollars a volume, and their ability to make beautiful books was not being utilized in any way.

Gilliss's suggestion was that we should bring them on to Garden City and establish a department of fine binding. After some negotiations this was accomplished. We purchased their tools, which as I remember numbered four thousand, and gave them an agreeable place in which to work in Garden City. From that time to this they have devoted themselves to making the most beautiful and perhaps the most extravagant leather bindings.

One of them died, and at this date there are only two left, Mr. Hardi and Mr. Pilon. They do a tremendous lot of work for the Metropolitan Museum of Art, and I think really have the cream of all the fine binding work done in this country. I also think that they do better work than anybody else in the field outside of France. In the end this department will pass away, but it will leave many examples of its superb skill.

Notwithstanding the fact that they charge what seem to me extraordinarily high prices, I do not think that the French binders have ever made a profit; it has cost us one or two thousand dollars a year all these years. But it has certainly been worth it to make this contribution to the arts—for it is, in my feeling, a real contribution—and I hope it will last for many days.

CHAPTER XXVII

THE LADY OR THE TIGER

I THINK I have mentioned in these pages the fact that authors are sometimes peculiar. Heaven forbid that I should strain this point; but there is one lady with whom I have had much to do and who has greatly distressed me. Her name is Ellen Glasgow, and she writes beautiful books; but she is about the hardest thing to get along with since Eve was made from Adam's rib.

She is the most cantankerous letter writer that the world has ever seen. In the first place, she writes in a hand that can be read only with the greatest difficulty; in the second place, her pen is dipped in blue vitriol; in the third place, it leaves a sting that is apt to last for a long time. She is a Southerner and a very charming woman when she behaves but, my Lord! how terrible she is when she does not behave.

I once received a letter from her which was so violent and unjust and generally cussed that while I was in a spirit of rebellion I went to see her.

She asked me to sit down beside her, which I declined to do. I said, "Ellen, you are behaving outrageously: that letter was perfectly unreasonable and crazy and I am not going to stand it; and unless you make a contract with me in writing to behave yourself in future, you can take your books and go to blazes."

I never expected to see her again, but much to my surprise she sweetly began: "Effendi, you treat me as if you were a cave man. Don't you know that that is the way women love to be treated?"

I told her that I did not, and thereupon wrote out an agreement that she was to behave, and she signed it. It read as follows:

> I will be good. You manage my book in the way you think best and I won't interfere until you prove that you have not done the proper thing, so help me Bob.

This was put away with our contracts, but it has not been of excessive value.

She was rather a pretty woman, and she needed to be. Her word lasted a month or two, and within a short time I had another letter fairly screeching with ill nature. And yet she is not so bad, either, and at times I am fond of her when she does not have her claws out. When she does have them out, I would rather face a wild tiger.

She came to me one time and told me that she was going to have Mr. Brett* publish her next book. I told her by no means to do this—that she would never get along with Mr. Brett, as they were entirely different in their characteristics.

Notwithstanding, of course, she did give her book to Mr. Brett. I was down South somewhere and received a

* George P. Brett of the Macmillan Company.

long telegram from her demanding that I return at once to New York and get this book away from Mr. Brett, and expressing the greatest surprise that I should have permitted her to make such a foolish mistake—she could hardly forgive me.

We still have these experiences with this gifted author. I sometimes wish that she wrote less well in producing books and more pleasantly in producing letters. There is one consolation, as I said before: she writes such a terrible hand that it is impossible to read most of the insults, but you can bet your life they are there.

CHAPTER XXVIII

THE NORRIS FAMILY

It is very rare for a whole family to start to write successful books. There may be other instances of it, but the only ones that I recall are the books of the Norris family, turned out and still turned out in such liberal numbers.

I think that Frank Norris came to us when we were still Doubleday & McClure Company, and I can remember his desk in the general office where he read many manuscripts; and I am not sure but that he wrote some portions of his novels in that room. He had come from San Francisco, where he had been a free lance, working largely on a paper called the *Wave*. Just exactly how he connected himself with the Doubleday & McClure Company, I cannot at the moment recall, but I do remember that he produced a book called *Blix*, which I think was his first book* and which was run as a sort of filler in a San Francisco weekly. It had much to commend it, and we published it in 1899 with moderate success. It was the

---

* Actually, it was his third. *Moran of the Lady Letty* and *McTeague* were published before *Blix*.

beginning of a relationship which lasted as long as Frank Norris lived.

He was a striking personality, open in character and extraordinary in appearance. At the age, I think, of twenty-six or twenty-eight his hair was snow white and abundant. He was only thirty-two when he died of appendicitis in San Francisco. Curiously enough, his wife had the same disease at the same time, but recovered.

He had just begun to make his way as an author and was highly esteemed as a manuscript reader when he decided to get married to a girl who was living in California. He came in one day and said, "Mr. Doubleday, with your permission I propose to get married."

"When?" I asked.

"That is up to you," he replied; "it depends on the salary you are willing to give me."

We discussed this delicate subject for some time and arranged for a salary which we hoped he might live on with more or less comfort. I remember that we loaned him the use of our house on Sixteenth Street for one summer, which helped out.

He thereupon telegraphed his best beloved some money and told her to take the train and come right on; and he was married in St. George's Church, I being the third person present.

We always had a deep affection for Norris, and he was ever an intimate associate. I think he would have done very great things had he lived. As it was, he left a record for a man so young which was really extraordinary, and he had in his head plans for even greater books which I know would have materialized had he lived.

A few years before his death his brother, Charles G. Norris, came to us as a clerk, and was associated with us, I think, for several years. At that time he had never written anything, so far as I know, and never expected to; but suddenly, after he had left us to become one of the assistant editors of the *American Magazine,* he gave up his job and began to write novels. At first I think it was pretty hard, but he certainly worked at the task with extraordinary energy, and finally produced books which were most successful and achieved large sales.

Sometime before he commenced to write, his wife, Kathleen Norris, blossomed out as a novelist. The first notable thing that she did, I think, was the book called *Mother,* which Theodore Roosevelt characterized as a really magnificent influence. It was advertised far and wide. Edward Bok, of the *Ladies' Home Journal,* regarded *Mother* so well that he published it in his magazine when the book had been already published for a year or two.

When I consider what luck we had, I sometimes think that a special Providence watched over us. When *Mother* was offered to us, Harry Lanier, one of our partners, thought that it was not good enough to be printed in book form, so the manuscript was declined. Mrs. Norris took it to Macmillan's, who accepted it, and I think sold about thirty or forty thousand copies. She then came to us and asked if we would not take it over, which was an extraordinary exhibition of good nature after what had happened. We told her that we would do so with pleasure, and I believe we sold over one hundred thousand copies.

This was the first of a long list of books written by the Norris family. They gradually increased in circulation and became better and better known until now, I think, sixty or seventy thousand copies of each new book are sold. The whole Norris story is very different from anything that I have ever heard of before, and I am very glad to be associated with it for every reason, personal and financial.

CHAPTER XXIX

GENE STRATTON PORTER

Mr. Richard Watson Gilder, the editor of the *Century Magazine,* once did me a great favor, and I am sure he knew he was doing it at the time, which made it all the more gracious, coming, as it did, from a competitor. He had received the manuscript of a book on some nature subject, written by a Gene Stratton Porter, of Geneva, Indiana. He wrote to the author that the book was very good, but not in his line, and highly recommended that it should be submitted to Doubleday, Page & Company.

In due time the manuscript of a book called *Freckles* came to us, and was at first a matter of much discussion. I was going away to Nassau, in the Bahamas, when Mr. Lanier handed me this manuscript and asked me to read it. I remember that I did read it under a palm tree and thought very highly of its popular character, and cabled Mr. Lanier that I was sure if we took this book we would sell large editions.

This was the beginning of our relationship with Gene Stratton Porter. We published the book and sold, I think, eight or ten thousand copies; but later, when it was put in a Grosset & Dunlap reprint, it sold, I think, more than a couple of million.

I went out to see Mrs. Porter in Geneva and found her a very delightful and simple person, who loved nature and had written this book more because she was interested in outdoor life than to make a successful novel. For twenty-five years we published her books, some of them devoted to nature subjects, and many of them devoted, as of course everyone knows, to nature fiction. We became very close friends, and every second year she would produce a novel, which we published on her birthday, August 17. We would sell in advance anywhere from one to two hundred thousand copies, and she has always been our most popular author.

Her interest in the concern was deep and affectionate. She felt like one of the partners herself, and was always eager to help in any plan we ever undertook. About two years ago [December 1924] she was killed in a trolley accident, and we lost a friend whom we can never replace; but our relations still continue with her daughter, and the sales of her books show that their real value was not over-estimated, as they go on selling still in large numbers.

We were very anxious to introduce Gene Stratton Porter's nature fiction into England, although we did not consider it surprising, since her books were entirely American and dealt with American flowers, moths, and the whole round of nature subjects, that they should not interest English readers. We had succeeded in selling Mr. Murray* small editions of perhaps a thousand or two,

* Of John Murray, Publishers, Ltd., later Sir John Murray.

which seemed to satisfy him. One day when I was in his office in London I said:

"Do you realize that you could sell a hundred thousand copies of Gene Stratton Porter's popular novels of which you now sell a thousand or two?"

He said that he did not.

"If you will try the plan of window displays such as we use in America," I said, "I am sure you can get great results."

We at once sent over copies of material which we had used for displays and to get publicity in the newspapers. He followed our plan and made a cheap edition of *Freckles* at a shilling or two. The book instantly responded; I am not quite sure, but I think he sold eventually between half a million and a million copies.

We had much the same experience with O. Henry. I tried to induce an English publisher to take him up, and I remember, among others, talking to William Heinemann and urging him to read the O. Henry books. This he did, and his only comment was that I might just as well ask him to read a book in Greek; he did not understand the slang, nor did he care for the style of the author, or anything about the books. Eventually, O. Henry was taken up by Hodder & Stoughton.

I think the first person to give any publicity to O. Henry was Sir James Barrie. He sent some of the books to the Prime Minister, who remarked that they were a sure cure for all affairs of state when they became burdensome at night. Somehow this was published in the newspapers and so started the ball rolling.

At that time huge circulations were secured for popular

books at very low prices, even as little as seven pence per copy. Apparently the people who bought books of this type were just the kind of people who appreciated O. Henry. The volume of his success in England was always a surprise to me. I think more than a million copies of O. Henry's books were sold there. How the British reader ever understood O. Henry's subtle charm is beyond me; but we accepted our good luck, as we had done before and have done since. Hodder & Stoughton have just published two new editions in a little more expensive and more attractive format. Here, again, is a publishing experience which I am unable to explain.

CHAPTER XXX

CHRISTOPHER MORLEY

THE STORY of the association with Chris Morley is, I fear, a chestnut, because he printed the story as a preface in one of his books, I think *Tales from a Rolltop Desk*. But I always am delighted to think back over our pleasant experiences, which began the first day I ever saw him and have never ceased.

One morning a young man blew into our Garden City office and I think first met Arthur Page; perhaps he had a letter of introduction to him, I am not sure. At all events, he said he was a Rhodes scholar and had to have a job. Arthur did not have anything for him and suggested that the best thing he could do would be to go back to New York, and offered to show him the way to the train.

Morley declined the invitation and said he would stick around for a while. He then began to investigate and ask questions about who was who. Finally he learned that a man named F. N. Doubleday was the president of the company, asked where his office was, and walked in on me with a bright and smiling face. He said he had told Mr. Page that he was a Rhodes scholar. I think he felt that that was the strongest introduction he could have, and perhaps it was. He had to have a job, he said, and he had to have it right away.

I asked him what he meant by "right away," and he said, "Before twelve o'clock."

"Aren't you a little swift on the trigger?" I inquired.

"No," he replied; "I have got to have it because I have certain expenses to pay, and you can give it to me now as well as later."

We had quite a long talk, and I found that he had a very good knowledge of literary values and a lot of ideas, some of which I thought were good and some of which I thought were no good. Finally, with the idea of drawing him out, I said to him:

"If you could have any job in this place, what job would you take?"

He instantly replied, "Yours."

"All right," I said; "I will give you a chance to get it," and I found a desk for him and told him to proceed to work his way into the organization.

As everyone knows, he was a delightful addition to our staff and was with us several years until he decided to go into writing for himself, and I think became a newspaper-man on the Philadelphia *Ledger*. From that day to this his success has been increasingly great, until his latest book, *Thunder on the Left,* has reached a sale of nearly one hundred thousand.

I hope he feels toward Doubleday, Page & Company as Doubleday, Page & Company feel toward him. Our association has always been of the closest, and I hope always will be.

CHAPTER XXXI

"ELIZABETH AND HER GERMAN GARDEN"

OF ALL the charming women that I have met in the publishing business—and there have been at least a hundred thousand—Lady Russell,* who writes under the name of the "Author of 'Elizabeth and Her German Garden,'" stands very high. I have known her for many years, and extremely well.

In 1919, just after the war, I was in London. "Elizabeth" had just married Earl Russell and was about to go through those experiences which are truthfully described in *Vera*. She was anxious to get back to Germany to see her old garden and the people with whom she had lived as a neighbor for so many years. She said that if Florence and I would take her back just to have a look, she would write a beautiful book for us entitled, *X Y Z Revisits*

* Lady Russell was Mary Beauchamp of Sydney, Australia. She married the Graf von Arnim, who died in 1910, and in 1916 she married Earl Russell, the brother of Bertrand Russell.

Germany. That seemed a very attractive subject to me, and we agreed to make the journey.

Of all the disagreeable, hard, upsetting trips that I have ever made, this was the worst. The trains were dirty and crowded beyond endurance. It took twenty-four hours or more to reach Berlin from Ostend. All through the night the conductors would come through and ask for tickets which we did not have, and money of which we never had the right sort, and it was every minute a hectic and unpleasant affair. I was crowded up against "Elizabeth," as we both had to sleep sitting up, and I felt a very hard substance, which I thought must be a bottle, pressing against my leg. I asked her what she had hung around her waist. She said it was a bottle of chloroform.

"For heaven's sake, what for!" I exclaimed.

She said, "I thought that you and Florence might get in trouble in Germany and this would be a convenient thing to have around."

I found that she had carried this bottle hung around her waist, ever since we started, knocking it on whatever she might fall against, and thanked my stars that the cork did not come undone and we were not all suffocated.

When we got to Berlin we could not get any accommodations at all. We finally worked our way into a hospital where we slept the first night. Then we could not get accommodations back to London except by bribing a German physician to give us a paper indicating that Mrs. Doubleday had a case of nervous prostration and Lady Russell was her nurse, and we had to get back to England for the sake of our health. Thus, in due course, we got out of Germany alive.

But not before "Elizabeth" went to her old home, which was a wreck of its former glory. The gardens were gone and everything that was attractive had disappeared with the war. She showed extraordinary nerve, and never for a moment gave way to her feelings, whatever they were.

The book was never written. She told Florence that she had planned the story that I should run away with her, and she (Florence) was to run away with Maximilian Harden. The chance of such a book ever being put down on paper was very remote, and thus we missed a good seller.

I am quite convinced that "Elizabeth" was very fearful that she would get into trouble when she arrived in Germany. She thought that they would probably be deeply offended at her action, and she was very anxious not to see any more people than she could help. But one of the first persons we ran across was Professor Bonn, who at that time was in the Foreign Office. I have forgotten under what name we introduced "Elizabeth," because Professor Bonn was supposed not to know who she was. He did know, instantly, but he did not show that he had any information about her, and I think she felt greatly relieved.

Sometime during the war there appeared a book called *Christine,* evidently written by "Elizabeth." It was in exactly her style and manner so that a mistake seemed impossible. We had a contract with her for her next book, but *Christine* had been given to Macmillan. I charged her with going back on her agreement, but she wrote me that this book was not hers; that she had never seen or heard of it until I called it to her attention, when she sent out and bought a copy and read it, and she hoped that her literary style was not "so unbuttoned" as the style in which this book was written. She further authorized me to contradict reports that she had anything to do with the book, which I did; but nobody believed her, least of all ourselves.

In London one day she drew me aside from her husband, Lord Russell, and told me that even he, as a matter of fact, did not know that she had written the book, and it came about through the request of Mr. Brett that she should write a book on a plan which he had conceived. She said that she did not feel at liberty to take his idea and turn over the book to us, so she had to go on with Mr. Brett.

When we were in London at the beginning of 1919, "Elizabeth" came with her husband, Lord Russell, to pay a call on us. Florence took a great dislike to Russell, but "Elizabeth" wanted to talk business with me, so we left Florence to the tender mercies of his lordship.

When we returned, "Elizabeth" asked much to our surprise: "Have you a bathroom here at Brown's connecting with your other room?"

We told her that we had. She said: "Can I come and take a bath? My geyser is broken."

So we treated her to a hot bath, which she regarded as a luxury. Lord Russell was eager to get one, too, but we called a halt on that.

"Elizabeth's" troubles with Russell were never ending. He was the worst hound that I have known for many years. We were glad to see the last of him, and I am sure "Elizabeth" was, too. She refused to divorce him, so he cannot remarry. Having had three wives, "Elizabeth" thought that was enough for him.

CHAPTER XXXII

BOOTH TARKINGTON

VERY EARLY in our publishing history we had the manuscript of a novel submitted to us through a sister of Booth Tarkington, of whom at that time we had never heard. It was called *The Gentleman from Indiana* and I think had been declined by Harper's. Sam McClure was instantly taken with it, and we agreed to publish it serially and in book form, with the results which are now well known.

Tarkington was one of the shyest birds I have ever known. He was so shy, indeed, that he preferred to have his sister do the business with the publisher, so we came to know her almost better than the author himself.

I remember that I took a great fancy to him from the first moment I ever saw him—admiration which has continued up to this moment. He was tall and nervous, and as I recall lived on the fifth floor of a boardinghouse on Madison Avenue. Fortunately, the writer of an autobiography has no modesty whatever, so nothing interferes with putting in anything which is disgracefully egotistical,

[203]

and I am copying a letter which he wrote to me about this boardinghouse:

Twenty-five Years After

One morning, about a quarter of a century ago, a thin young man with a large nose came out of his hall-bedroom, on the top floor of a Madison Avenue boardinghouse, and, leaning over the railing of the stairway well, listened with joy to the slow ascent of a visitor. There were six flights of stairs, the steepest in New York, and though the ascending gentleman could not be seen, he could be heard to pant, to puff and to blow laboriously on his way. Now, giving ear to such ascents was one of the pleasures of living at the top of that tall and narrow house; moreover, the thin young man, aged about twenty-seven, had made an engagement, a day or so before, with a fat and luxurious youthful clergyman, who was to call for him at this hour, and was naturally supposed by the thin young man to be the ascending grampus—for truly like a grampus did the climber inhale and exhale the troublous air. Sometimes a suffocated groan was heard, sometimes a heavy sigh and even sounds like mutterings; whereupon, at every such token of suffering, the thin young man would double himself in silent laughter. Then upon the topmost flight appeared, not the expected rotund figure but another, that of a tall man a little older than the watcher, like the latter in having a large nose, but unlike him in every other item of appearance. He was a man who would have done well with a ruff in a portrait of Van Dyke's, or as a captain of mousquetaires in one of the romantic plays that held the stage that year;— and at sight of him, the thin young man became weak with horror, for he had sent down word: "Tell the gentleman to come up," instead of descending himself to the communal parlor. He had done this in order to give himself the pleasure of hearing his fat friend suffer on the long climb; and here, instead, was the very last person in the world whose temper he wished to test. For the thin young man was a rejected writer and throughout five interminable years he had met unabated rebuff, while the caller was the senior member of the firm that had just accepted his first novel. What he expected to hear was a few simple words of destruction: "Since you're too important to come down, but make *me* risk my limbs and lungs on these stairs instead, you're certainly too important for me to publish! Kindly bring a wheelbarrow to the office at three this afternoon and remove your manuscript."

The course followed by the pubisher was not as anticipated. When he got his breath he invited the young man to a little dinner for Kipling. Such is Effendi.

He could get up those stairs now as well as ever. I ran up and down them without a thought those days; I should ask for a rope and basket now, but Effendi changes little. Perhaps this is partly because his life and his work have been so prodigiously successful—success is a grand tonic!—but I think it is mainly due to what we call the disposition of the man. Long ago I made note of a peculiarity of his. When he was angry I noticed that he looked amused.

I mean that when he had reason to be angry, when, as we say, the world seemed to be going wrong, or when, perhaps, he was assailed, his expression became humorous; one that may carry its owner a long way, and that also preserves his health. Add to it the long-headed clarity of his thinking, and his capacity to carry not only broad outlines but innumerable details in his mind—well, such a combination is "hard to stop"; and it is even harder to stop when it has behind it the extraordinary, the rather hidden sheer force of Effendi. And yet all this is not the greatest part of him; that is his feeling toward his fellow men. For Effendi is an Effendi of the tribe of Abou Ben Adhem.

Tarkington was always a good-natured sort of chap, and if anybody wanted a book by him, he wanted to give it to him. We had the utmost difficulty in keeping him within boundary lines; in fact, he gave Harper two or three books which we deeply regret we have not got now.

Russell [Doubleday] about this time took up the job of cultivating him and keeping in the closest touch; otherwise we never would have had any books by him, as he would have given them to perfect strangers if they had asked him for them. Fortunately, Russell was able gradually to work him into camp, and I am sure now that he is ours for keeps. We have done well with his books, made two or three special editions, and I think he is abundantly satisfied—at all events he is a delightful man to do business with, and we get along well with his wife, who is a good businesswoman. His work gets better and better, and I am sure his books will live.

CHAPTER XXXIII

THE MAN OF MYSTERY, COLONEL HOUSE

I FIRST MET Colonel House* in 1918, at the very height of his power. I had been to China and Japan on a mission for the Red Cross, and in Japan I had met the Prime Minister and the Minister for Foreign Affairs. There were certain things which the Foreign Minister was anxious to express to the President in the way of explaining why Japan had difficulty with the plan of negotiating treaties in the open. At that time Wilson was very eager to have everything diplomatic done in the public view. This elaborate explanation the Foreign Minister thought I could give the President verbally much better than it could be written, so he went over this whole subject with great care and asked me to convey his main ideas to the President.

When I got to Washington I saw [the President's secretary, Joseph P.] Tumulty and told him the circum-

* Edward Mandell House, a close associate of President Woodrow Wilson.

stances, and he promised to make an appointment with the President. The war was still on, it will be remembered, in the late spring of 1918. I could not see the President and was finally told to see Colonel House, who had full authority to do anything necessary in connection with the message from the Foreign Minister of Japan.

So for the first time I came to meet the Colonel. He was living that summer at Manchester-by-the-Sea on the north coast of Massachusetts, and I went there to see him. He was charming and cordial, and took all the time that was necessary to receive my message, to thoroughly understand and comment on it. I felt that I had done as well as I should have done if I had seen the President, and I was much impressed at that time with the closeness of his associations with Washington, D.C. He had a private wire that ran underground all the way from Washington into his library at Manchester-by-the-Sea.

I came to know him well, and he gave me several jobs in the way of publicity to attend to which I did my best to carry out—as I look back on it, without any special success. It was an awfully fussy affair getting things into the newspapers which they did not want to print, or not giving them things which they did want to print. This started an acquaintance, if not an actual friendship, which has lasted through the years, and I have known him more or less intimately ever since. Of course, we wanted to get his book, and my experiences in this connection I have never been able to understand.

House came to see us quite often at Oyster Bay, sometimes spending the week end. One day he asked me to come aside with him privately in my den, as he wanted to talk with me about his memoirs.

"Effendi," he said, "I want you to be my literary executor."

I told him that I might decide to "go west" [die] first, in which case it would make it awkward.

"Well, if you do," he replied, "we will make some other arrangement, but I should like to have you take charge of my papers and publish my book."

We had a long confab on the subject, and I offered to advance him a thousand dollars a month while the book was in preparation, and help him to put it in shape. He complained of not having much money, but he said he did not need the advance then—if he did, he would let me know—so I regarded the matter as settled.

Later he went to Mr. [Cyrus] Curtis, of the *Saturday Evening Post* and the Philadelphia *Ledger,* and talked to him in much the same way. He arranged to contribute his memoirs to the *Post,* and to give Scribner's or [George] Doran the book—I have forgotten which. I think every publisher in New York claimed that they had the book at one time or another during the years when the matter was under discussion.

I saw him often at other times, and talked over further details of his memoirs. Afterwards I learned that he had talked, as I have said, with other publishers in exactly the same way. I remember he spent a week end with us when Conrad was visiting, and he was delightful and amusing and told Conrad a great many entertaining stories.

Gradually the plan of publishing a book seemed to fade from his mind, and finally he told us that he had put the papers in the hands of Yale University, which we supposed meant simply for preservation. It was a surprise to us, therefore, when he announced that he had made arrangements with Professor Seymour to prepare his memoirs, and that he would sell the syndicate [rights] to the highest bidder. We were not even invited to make a bid for the syndication, although he had assured me over and over again that we were to be treated with every consideration.

Finally, as everybody knows, the papers were edited, I think in a more or less careless way, by his college professor friend, and published through the *Tribune*. I am told that the syndication brought nearly two hundred thousand dollars, and afterwards, as we know, the material was published in book form. I think Houghton Mifflin, who issued the book, printed a first edition of fifty thousand copies and sold only about twenty thousand, so there was no reason for our being jealous.

Just after the announcement Colonel House came to dinner with us and I charged him with perfidy in telling me that he was going to give us the book and then taking it elsewhere. He said that we had too many war books to give this the attention it required, so he had given it to Houghton Mifflin, who did not have any war books at all (so he said). As a matter of fact, the whole thing was very cloudy and queer. One might have expected this sort of thing from a literary man, but not from a diplomat.

In the spring of 1926 we met again in London, where he was being entertained by the swells just as if he had as much power as he had in the old Wilson days. He is a remarkable man whom I confess I do not understand at all. I suppose the thing came out as well as it could, because we should not have been willing to print the things he said about [Ambassador] Page, and perhaps he, too, had˙this in the back of his mind.

There were many cruel things said of him, and I think his reputation toward the end of his career suffered a relapse, which was a pity, because as a man of mystery he was a great success, and his experiences were different and more extraordinary than any experiences that ever happened to any other man along the lines that he followed. In England they called him the Empty House and his wife the Vacant Lot, which was pretty tough, but still he is regarded with respect abroad, and somehow manages to keep in with the powers that be—a curious man and a curious experience.

CHAPTER XXXIV

WILLIAM HEINEMANN
AND
WILLIAM HEINEMANN, LTD.

Of all the strange things that have happened to me, I think well along toward the top of the list was my acquaintance with William Heinemann and what came of it. As mentioned in another chapter, I had great respect for Mr. Heinemann's literary judgment. He was an extraordinary man, and I think not very happy. I feel sorry to look back on what I know must have been times of real suffering and depression. I had known him for nearly thirty years, and usually disagreed with him on every subject, yet we maintained a curious kind of friendship and saw each other fairly often when I was in London or he was in New York. Our acquaintance, as I say, did not always run smoothly, we so often found ourselves on opposite sides of many questions.

For instance, I was anxious to make with him a complete set of Conrad, and I worked out the plan as carefully and effectively as I could. When I presented it to him he

infuriated me by saying that it was merely "book furniture," sold to ignorant people to fill up their library shelves
and make it appear that they had some cultivation. This
was a disappointment and I left his office in a huff, but
we made it up afterwards and eventually carried out the
Sundial Edition.

Heinemann was a German Jew with a curious mixture
of English ideas and customs, German ideas and customs,
and Jewish ideas and customs. I think he was quite un-
popular with his own people; he was extremely irritable
and had no gift of co-operation. His closest associate was
his partner, Sydney S. Pawling, who had started the business with him in 1898. Apparently, as nearly as I could see,
Pawling hated the very sight of Heinemann, and yet they
were partners together for thirty years.

He had a faculty for picking the best and the worst
books in the literary market. A glance at the Heinemann
catalogue shows how clever he was, and his business, I
think, was always highly successful from the literary point
of view and fairly profitable from the money end.

That I should ever succeed him as chairman of the
Heinemann business seems to me, as I look back at it, the
most unlikely thing in the world, and yet this came about.
Florence, Patty,* Nelson, and I were all in London in the
fall of 1920. We had a dinner date with Heinemann within
a day or two of our arrival in town. His dinners were
artistic creations in every sense, both culinary and intellectual, and we looked forward with pleasure to his enter-
tainments. We were shocked and horrified on going to

---

* Martha Nicholson Doubleday, the first wife of Nelson Doubleday, Sr.

his office the next morning to find a notice posted on the door: he had died during the night. It was really an accident; he had fallen on the floor and struck his head, having entangled his foot in a blanket, and no one being there he died from brain congestion.

Of course, everything was immediately in all sorts of disorder, but as our relationship was only semisocial, we were not particularly concerned in the business of the organization. Pawling was very much upset. He owned forty-five per cent of the Heinemann stock and Heinemann owned the controlling interest of fifty-five per cent; but each partner had the option of buying out the other at book value in case of death. Pawling was afraid that someone would get hold of Heinemann's stock and, having control, would oust him from his position. This seemed to be very likely. I asked him if there was anything we could do to help him, and he said that it would be ideal if we would buy out Heinemann's interest, working through the Pawling option.

I was instantly struck with the value of the suggestion, told him that I saw no reason why we should not do this, and practically agreed in five minutes to take Heinemann's stock—an impulsive action which was far from sensible but entirely successful in the end.

Before we left London we had legally obligated ourselves to buy Heinemann's controlling interest. Pawling was much concerned that someone would hear about it, and he said if it were known that the Heinemann business was owned by Americans, it would ruin the enterprise. This seemed to me a little tough, but we came away with the understanding that we would finance the business with whatever new capital was needed.

All our people in Garden City enthusiastically approved, although it was rather a risky affair, since we knew nothing of the English publishing business and had had little association with any of the partners except Pawling.

It is interesting to me to look back on the situation in which we found ourselves, controlling a business without any experience either in that particular line or in English business generally. Of course, it is very simple to think of an English business looking in from the outside, but very different controlling the business and looking from the inside out. We found the strangest things, or at least they appeared strange to us. For instance, the chief confidential books of the accounting department were kept in the chartered accountant's office in the City, miles from [Heinemann's offices in] Bedford Street, and even the head cashier and bookkeeper knew little or nothing of the final figures of profit and loss each year.

The Heinemann banking relations were curious to the last degree. They had banked with one institution for thirty years, but had never been able to borrow any money from the bank, and had kept an absurdly small balance—I think when we took over the business it was about one hundred and fifty pounds.

I thought the first thing to do was to introduce some sort of bookkeeping system upon which we could rely, and we sent over Larry McNaughton to give them the benefit of all the information that we had on that subject.

One tragedy followed another. Within a year and a half

Mr. Pawling was taken ill and died, so we had to buy out his stock interest as well as Heinemann's, ending in our full ownership of the whole enterprise. It became known at once that we were the owners of the business, and so far as I could see, it did no harm. I do not think we lost a single author.

We increased the wages of our staff; remodeled and rejuvenated the accounting system so that we knew where we stood; we sent the heads of our Garden City departments on a visit to England to tell them everything that we knew and brought the heads of departments of the English concern to Garden City to show them how we did business. The result, I think, was quite remarkable; it brought a feeling of friendliness which has accomplished wonderful things.

Quite naturally, I think, the Heinemann staff was suspicious of us; they thought that we would be efficient to the point of the dagger, cut salaries, lengthen hours, and be mean in our point of view, causing everyone to work harder for less money. It did not take long, I am thankful to say, after we had increased the pay of everybody in the building, to overcome this unfortunate state of things, and profits immediately began to mount, because instead of personal hostility one to another, we began to get co-operation not only in the London staff but with our staff in Garden City.

I cannot but be thankful, as well as happy, to remember what a short time it took for us firmly to establish confidence and friendships in all the employees in Bedford Street. We did not discharge a single person, nor did we hire a single American, and I believe that this is true to the present time. I give the greatest credit to the managers, Theodore Byard and Charles S. Evans, Oliver, Reeves, and all the rest of them, for developing the situation in such a friendly and effective way. So far as I can remember, we have never given them any order to do any one thing or not to do any one thing. They have worked with us hand and glove, so that no orders were necessary either way.

Mr. Byard had just been taken into the business to assist Heinemann in reading, being a good French, Italian, and German scholar. He had been a professional singer, and knew nothing about trade or business. After Pawling's death I was elected chairman, Byard was made vice-chairman, and Charley Evans secretary. Byard undertook to learn not only the technicalities of the publishing business but about business finance and business management generally. His interest was extraordinary; he would study and talk and work over business problems with me an unlimited number of hours every day. He helped to develop Oliver, the cashier, to get an expert outlook on the business and a knowledge of the daily maneuvers which were very valuable. I want to pay a tribute to him for his great effort and his successful mastery of a subject which was extremely difficult to encompass with his inexperience.

One day while Pawling was still alive but not really in his right mind, Evans told me that he could not get along with Pawling and proposed to go to Cassell, who had made him a liberal offer. I objected strongly to this, as I regarded his position as the key position in carrying on relations with authors. I had a hard time to convince him that he ought to stay and work with us, but I finally said, "Evans, if you will stay, I will guarantee that you will be happy and your wife will wear diamonds."

He put out his hand and said, "It is agreed," and I was glad to give his wife some diamonds as a souvenir when she was recently in the United States. He has worked with Byard in the closest and most friendly association, and has carried on the business in a way which has brought us fine results and I hope has given him pleasure and profit.†

I count myself fortunate in one visit that I made to "Elizabeth." She said, "Effendi, don't you want a bright young man who will be loyal and clever and useful in his job, whatever you put him at?"

I said I should be delighted. The result was that Frere Reeves came to call on me. I was immediately attracted to him and we had a little talk, and it was agreed that he should come and find a place to work himself into the business. His first job was in the magazine department, where he took up particularly the distribution of *Short Stories*. Here again was one of those English experiences which surprised me. *Short Stories* was and is, as I've written, American from top to bottom. Most of the slang is unintelligible to the English reader, yet Frere Reeves worked up the sale to something like thirty or forty thousand twice a month, and it carries the trifling loss that we still make on the English edition of *The World's Work*, now called *The World Today*.

This reminds me of a very bad thing that I did without thinking. Henry Roberts came to see us off at the steam-

† Mr. Evans was the father of A. Dwye Evans, currently chairman of Heinemann. The two publishing companies are no longer affiliated corporately.

ship train in London, and he told me almost with tears in his eyes that he could not sleep nights for worrying over *The World Today.*

I said, "Henry, sleep nights and keep awake in the day-time and you will be all right."

Before I realized what I had said the train pulled out. I am only hoping that Henry never got the words straight, and of course I did not mean anything unkind.

For twenty-five years we have run this English edition of *The World's Work.* It has been as low as seven thousand in circulation, and as high as ten thousand. We have changed the price up and down, and yet these seven thousand faithful people stick on, no matter how bad the magazine or how good. It is one of those extraordinary English notions of habit which I never can get quite used to.

I was much amused by being invited to lunch with one Jonathan Cape, whom I had never met. As I was extremely busy that week, I tried to get out of it, without success. We went to luncheon and nothing seemed to happen. Finally I said, "Mr. Cape, did you have any particular idea to discuss when you were good enough to invite me to this luncheon?"

"Yes," he said, "I did. You can hardly expect to make a success of your management of the Heinemann business; it will certainly fail, the conditions being entirely unfavorable, and I only want to tell you that, when you do fail, I stand ready to take it over."

I thanked him very kindly and told him that if it failed I would let him know. I have not communicated with him yet.

I was talking this over the other day with Christopher Morley, who thinks very highly of our friend. He claimed that it was simply a clever thing to do—that, if all went well, Cape lost nothing; but if I got into trouble with the Heinemann business, I would remember Cape's suggestion. I have no doubt Morley was correct, but it was perhaps a direct English way of working which I had not before experienced. It probably means that Mr. Cape will develop a business of large proportions and great success, as he seems to have that kind of dynamic mind.

Some of our Heinemann experiences were amusing—mostly leftover troubles from the old firm which we had to straighten out. Among others was the connection with the Loeb Library.

It seems that this enterprising man, Mr. Loeb, who made a fortune in the banking business and by marrying a rich woman (probably mostly by marrying the rich woman), had put up enough money to make the Loeb Library, but being canny, he planned that the public should pay as much as possible of this expense, and that his fame should go hurtling down the ages. I was never enthusiastic about this set of books, because the men who did the real work got little credit; and Loeb, who did nothing but furnish the difference between the receipts and the expenditures, plastered his name at the top of every advertisement and every book.

We found out that he had a contract with Heinemann personally, of which no one knew the details; it was in Gundry's safe in the City along with other private papers.

After Pawling's death we began to get things in order and find out just our position on a lot of difficult matters, and came across this contract. We finally found that Heinemann had been charging Loeb certain expenses which he had no right to charge.

Theodore Byard and Evans were thrown into a panic to discover this situation, especially as Loeb was about to send some relative to look over our books to see that we had done the right thing. The position was most embarrassing. I told Theodore to lay the whole story before Loeb and tell him we would do anything that he thought was right. This Theodore did, and Loeb thought it was right that we should pay all the money which Heinemann had charged in excess of the amount provided for in the contract. There was nothing to do but to accept his decision, and we had to pay, I think, something like three thousand pounds.

CHAPTER XXXV

SIDELIGHTS ON
THE ENGLISH BUSINESS

I HESITATE to speak of some interesting sidelights which I think were really rather significant; but as this is all among ourselves, it can do no harm.

Having been to England some twenty-five or thirty times, I thought I knew something about class feeling; but I soon found that I was grossly ignorant. I planned to start a Net Results Club in England such as we have in America, giving five per cent of the profits to certain heads of departments; and with the idea of introducing the subject, which I thought was a pleasant as well as a profitable one to all concerned, I invited five or six of the heads of departments to a dinner. I remember that Larry McNaughton, who was in England at the time, was present also.

I had a house on Green Street, London, that year, and after we had given them plenty of good food and champagne and something to smoke, I made the announcement, which I thought would be received with acclaim, that we would give five per cent of the profits each month in cash to the important members of the staff present, at a dinner to be provided where they could meet and talk about business and divide up the money equally.

Greatly to my surprise, a look of disapproval came over every face, and I could not imagine the reason why. It was so obvious that I let the matter drop and took up other things; and it was nearly a year before I unearthed the real trouble, which I thought extraordinary.

It seems that among these people there were various classes; one man regarded his social position as more important than that of another; and I finally discovered, after many conversations, that they objected to the whole scheme because everybody was put on the same basis. I was frankly appalled to discover this situation, but accepted it and said nothing; and the matter was dropped and no Net Results Club was started.

A year after that I was visiting London, and one of the men who was present at the dinner party came to me in a solicitous manner and said, "I suppose you thought we were a lot of fools that we didn't jump at the Net Results Club idea."

I said it was inadvisable for me to explain what I did think—why had he brought up the subject?

He said, "We have been talking it over and figuring what would have been gained if we had accepted your idea enthusiastically and helped you to put it over; and during these confidential talks we have become better acquainted with each other, and the business itself has brought us closer together. We now think that we made a great mistake not to have developed the idea with your help, and we would like to ask if you will renew your offer, because if you will we should like to start the Club."

The Club was started the next month and has been, I believe, a successful influence from that time to this.

One day Oliver, the cashier of the Heinemann company, in whose common sense I have great faith, said to me: "I would like to say something very personal, but I think important, if you would not be offended and would not regard it as an impertinence."

I told him that I should be more than delighted to hear anything that he had in his mind.

He then told me that in his opinion Great Britain was a nation of snobs. He said: "For instance, a man in a high position with a title would snub Mr. Pawling; Mr. Pawling, being the head of our business, would snub me; and I, being the head of a department, would snub my inferiors. I think it is important," he said, "that you should realize this, because it accounts for so much that otherwise you would not understand."

I have thought of this statement a thousand times, and rubbed my eyes to wonder if it were even partially true. I am thoroughly convinced that it was true at that time. The situation is getting better year by year, but the whole subject was a revelation to me, since I had not been clever enough to dig it out for myself.

Another experience which is very confidential happened before I had been in the business very long. A certain head of a department came into my office one morning in his usual respectful manner. According to custom, he would not take a chair unless I invited him to do so, so he stood before me and said that he had something private about which he wished to talk with me.

When I asked him what it was, he said that a certain head of another department had sent a messenger asking him to come and call upon him in his office in another part of the building. "I regard this as an impertinence," he said, "as my social position is infinitely superior to his."

"Sit right down," I said, "and I will go and see our friend and find out what he wants."

His embarrassment was naturally intense, but I forced him into a seat, went to see the man who had the suggestions to make, talked them over with him, and brought back the message to the department head who had been so touchy.

I never had that trouble afterwards. I really think that it could not happen now, but all these things helped me to understand why the English and the Americans so often see things queerly from each other's point of view.

Anybody who has visited Bedford Street remembers that the first floor is reached by some white marble steps and at the foot of these steps are folding doors. When I first became identified with the workings of the Heinemann business, these doors were always locked, and a visitor of any kind, important or unimportant, had to work his way through a little dark passage which looked like a coal hole. I objected to this and asked them why people should not use the proper marble steps and the doors be left open at the foot of them. The reply was that there was an overcoat stolen about thirty years before by a sneak thief who came up those same steps, and they did not want to lose another coat. I could hardly take this seriously, but

I found that it was understood seriously, and I only got the doors open for keeps by guaranteeing to pay for any overcoat or anything else that was stolen. Again, I am sure that I should not have the same trouble now, but it is a trifling example of how difficult it is to change an English custom, even when the reasons are obvious.

An example of the changed conditions in the Heinemann business is the Christmas dinner which they have every year now, attended by everybody in the shop from top to bottom. I think the last dinner included some eighty people and was a jolly affair—democratic and unconventional. A man in the packing room might be sitting next to Theodore Byard, etc., and all appearing on an equal basis. In a country of class distinctions like England this is quite remarkable—another example of what it means to have people interested primarily in accomplishing a given result. Certainly the Christmas dinner feature is always a pleasure to me to hear about. It reminds me of our own good will at Garden City.

One incident which came out well rather alarmed me at first. John Galsworthy was one of our best authors then, as he is now, and he was intensely antagonistic to the idea that an American should come in and purchase an English house in which his books were an important factor. He was a close friend of Mr. Evans, and advised him strongly, I think, to leave Heinemann's. He told Evans that the Americans cared only about the profit that they could make on books, and were unlikely to be successful or congenial with the staff.

But Evans, having started on his career with us and having thrown in his fortunes with the new Heinemann management, convinced Galsworthy that he should suspend judgment until he had had a little more experience. Charley Evans did warn me later that we were in danger of losing many of our best authors, should the statement gain currency that an American firm had taken over the Heinemann business and would introduce American efficiency methods and commercialize the whole concern.

I asked Charley who could help us most to put ourselves right with English authors, and he said Galsworthy. He suggested that Galsworthy and I should lunch together, when I could put my views before him and get his interest in our plans for the benefit of Heinemann's and all who dwelt therein.

I shall never forget that lunch as long as I live. It took place at the Automobile Club. I had just come off the deep and for almost the first time in my life had been deadly seasick; but the engagement was made and I was bound to keep it.

Galsworthy was delightful. I did not tell him what I lived through from course to course; every moment I feared would be my last, and that my stomach would do me in. Fortunately, I became so much interested in talking with Mr. Galsworthy about our plans, and he seemed so much interested in hearing of them, that I forgot about my stomach and dismissed it completely for the time being.

Much to my gratification—and I have never ceased to be thankful for it—Galsworthy seemed to think that our plans were not foolish, and one of the most important literary people in England has been a faithful and helpful friend from that day to this. His influence was of overwhelming importance and opened up a long train of friendships which I have enjoyed, especially in association with our London principals. I find it difficult to express, even to myself, the deep debt of gratitude that I owe to these many, many friends.

The only person I remember in all the list that we really lost was Hall Caine, and of all the bores and thick-headed idiots that I ever knew, he took the palm. His books were entirely out of key with the whole Heinemann business, but they had been very successful and the profits, I think, induced Heinemann with his thrifty mind to keep on with Hall Caine, especially as poor Pawling had to do all the dirty work.

I had several interviews with Caine, and Nelson did some talking, and we were both convinced that his material would be less valuable as time went on, and in any event would not add to the dignity or the quality of our list. He used to demand the most unreasonable things, and would worry everybody in the place for hours almost every day. Finally he received a proposition from Cassell to take over his books, and we were glad to accede to his suggestion. Thus Hall Caine's name came off the list, greatly to the improvement of the quality of the catalogue. So far as I know, he is the only author that we lost, notwithstanding all the talk of American domination, etc.

There is a great deal of discussion about England being in the depths of despair. It is not a matter that particularly concerns this manuscript, but I happened to read in the *Saturday Evening Post* a statement as to the increase of high incomes in connection with the income tax laws in England. I am copying the following paragraph, which seems to me very significant. The English capacity for going ahead in spite of all troubles seems overwhelming and very surprising, as I think these figures show:

The number having incomes from $25,000 to $50,000 a year was 9020 in 1914 and 16,589 in 1924, an increase of almost 84 per cent.

The number having incomes from $50,000 to $75,000 a year was 2393 in 1914 and 4353 in 1924, an increase of 82 per cent.

The number having incomes from $75,000 to $100,000 a year was 1002 in 1914 and 1828 in 1924, an increase of 82 per cent.

The number having incomes of $100,000 to $500,000 a year was 1513 in 1914 and 2763 in 1924, an increase of more than 82 per cent.

The number having incomes in excess of $500,000 a year was 80 in 1914 and 124 in 1924, an increase of more than 50 per cent.

It may be that popular government has been feeding the rich to the poor. Certainly taxation for social purposes has enormously increased. The government's expenditures for education, science and art were $100,000,000 in 1914 and $243,000,000 in 1925. Its expenditures for miscellaneous social services, health, labor and pensions in 1914 were $104,000,000, and in 1925 $720,000,000—that is to say, nearly seven times what they were before the war. The total expenditures under the head of poor-law relief by the state and local authorities in 1924 were $196,000,000.

What particularly surprised me was the changed conditions brought about by paying the Heinemann people decent salaries. I really believe that we do not appreciate how hard the conditions are for clerks and people of cultivation in England as compared with the situation that we know in the United States. A few shillings make an important difference in the pay of a man who is a clerk. Apparently, so far as the feeling goes, the extra money that we pay for services has been returned to us many times in co-operative friendly relations one with another; otherwise I do not see how we can account for practically doubling the business in a year or two, and I think more than doubling the profits. As a matter of fact, the records of the profits in the Heinemann days were so inadequate that it is almost impossible to draw any conclusions about the change brought about by the new conditions. Roughly speaking, we made in the first four years about seventy thousand pounds, of which about thirty thousand was used to charge off depreciation and for adjustments of various kinds which, with our severe ideas of bookkeeping, we thought were desirable. The moment we introduced the sort of figures which Larry prepares, which are probably almost too conservative, it seemed to have a good effect upon the whole business, making a target at which to shoot, and bringing out the finer aspects of marksmanship in the publishing business. At all events, the same quick instinct for new and good books has been preserved, and quite a distinguished publisher told me not long ago that our position in England was tremendously improved over what it was even in the Heinemann days, which I regarded as a great compliment, because Heinemann had a reputation for literary ability superior, I think, to that of almost any publisher in London. Charley Evans and Byard and the rest of them seem to be able to keep up the quality and advance the literary contents of the books and vastly improve them.

I could go on all day writing of my experience in England,* but before stopping I must include one last curious thing that happened.

One day in the spring of 1922 I was dressing, when a tremendous impression came over my mind which I have never been able to account for. My vision indicated that Pawling was sick and the whole Heinemann business in danger. I turned to Florence and said: "There is something the matter with Heinemann's; I think we had better take the next steamer and go over and find out what is wrong."

This we did, and I telegraphed in advance to Pawling, hoping that he would play golf with me.

When we arrived we found Byard, Charley Evans, and Henry Roberts waiting for us at the train in a state of excitement. They said that Pawling, who was at the moment in a nursing home, had acted very queerly and put everybody on the *qui vive,* and they felt that they could not undertake to go on in the situation in which they found themselves; namely, that Pawling had the authority to order anything he chose, and they could not induce him to change his point of view, which they thought indicated nothing

---

* In 1910, Mr. Doubleday wrote (though few of his colleagues knew it) *A Plain American in England,* signing it "Charles T. Whitefield." This was a charming, tongue-in-cheek account of life among the British "swells."

The more he went to England, Effendi wrote, the more he believed they were "the finest people in the world." In fact they were so nice, he added, that when he said as much to his English friends, they were too polite to contradict him.

short of madness. They said that they had been trying to get up their nerve to telegraph me, but had not done so, fearing it would be disloyal to Pawling. Evidently they sent us some mental wirelesses which took effect and registered in my brain.

This was a hard visit. Pawling was in a nursing home under the care of Sir Thomas Horder, and he insisted upon holding his position, which he obviously could not manage. I had to make some arrangement by which he should not be allowed the authority to do things which might wreck the business and in time surely would have done so. In addition, the chief men of the shop were up in arms and unwilling to go on under Pawling's administration.

We finally worked it out, and made an arrangement through Sir Thomas Horder—who acted like a trump and really saved the business—by which Pawling could be kept from doing harm; at all events until he had thoroughly recovered.

The poor chap got worse and worse, and died the following December. All this was a great blow to me, because when the suggestion that we should buy the business first came up, I looked upon it as a splendid opportunity for Pawling to get the benefit of his years of labor, while helping to carry on in association with us in a successful way for all concerned. But it was not to be.

CHAPTER XXXVI

ENGLISH BANKING
EXPERIENCES

I WAS much interested in finding out how the English do business with the banks. As I have said, I was inexperienced, and I certainly did not achieve success with the Heinemann bank, which had no use for the publishing business in general and Heinemann in particular; so, accompanied by Nelson, I went to see my old friends, Brown, Shipley & Company, with whom we have had an account for twenty-five years. Their office is in Founders Court, a black little alley down in the City, where the maximum amount of business is conducted with the minimum amount of space and comfort. I asked to see Mr. Brown, Jr., and had no difficulty in getting invited into his office. I told him about our purchase of the Heinemann business, and asked him if it would be agreeable to lend us ten thousand pounds with the understanding that we would return it at the rate of a thousand pounds a month. He said, "Perfectly," and treated me, as they always have treated me, with delightful cordiality. At the time of the outbreak of the war, when we had notified Pinker not to draw on us when exchange was out of sight, the Brown, Shipley people had accepted our draft just the same, saying that they could not have Doubleday, Page & Company's name dishonored even for a few hours.

When we came to make the arrangement for giving the notes for the ten thousand pounds, they handed me a printed form containing, I should think, some three or four hundred words. I was rather embarrassed, because I did not like to sign the printed form without reading it, and I did not like to read it because Mr. Brown said it was the form that they had used for twenty years.

I asked him to excuse me for a minute to let me read it, which he did; but one of the paragraphs I found entirely unintelligible from my point of view. I think it bound me to do things which were not clearly stated.

I asked Mr. Brown what that particular paragraph meant. He looked at it seriously and read it all through, and said: "I really cannot tell you. I haven't read one of these notes for a score of years."

He sent for his man in the legal department—who was out to lunch. Finally he got one of the cashiers, who read it all through, and could not understand or explain it any better than Mr. Brown.

We were about to give it up when the banker said: "Suppose we cut it out. Will that be satisfactory to you?"

"Perfectly," I said, and this was done.

As an example of banking habit, it was nicely ironic when you consider that probably many millions and millions of pounds had been negotiated on that form, which nobody had read for fifteen or twenty years.

Another thing that surprised me was that accounts were kept in huge books about two feet square and with a thousand pages—terribly clumsy and inconvenient affairs in every way. I asked Mr. Brown why they did not use the card system, and he said it was against the law; the banking rules required that the records should be kept in books of a prescribed type, notwithstanding the tremendous inconvenience. It is one of the hundred examples of the old traditional habits of the English mind. They are making constant advances and changes now, I think, but they certainly have a long way to go.

I then went to see the Equitable Trust Company people and asked them if they would lend us ten thousand pounds, which they said they would be delighted to do. Then I went to the English department of the National City Bank and put my same question there, and they accepted my invitation with politeness and real enthusiasm. I was tremendously bucked up to find out what a good reputation we had and how easy it was to borrow money, even on long term—because I told them that it would take us more than a year or two to work out all these loans completely. I am thankful to say that the Heinemann people paid back the loans as rapidly as promised and we were soon out of debt. The latter experience was a particularly pleasant and satisfactory one to me, as it showed the large-minded friendliness of the American bank in a foreign city, even when the money was loaned to a foreign concern.

CHAPTER XXXVII

AMERICAN BOOKS
IN ENGLAND

A CURIOUS EXPERIENCE with book sales occurred in connection with the *Life of Henry Ford* and his recent book,
Today and Tomorrow. Both books I regard as extraordinary. The sales as noted, have been very moderate in this
country; we have never been able to get the books off their
feet. I presume it is because once Mr. Ford made an ass
of himself with a Peace Ship, and it was not helped
when he was on the witness stand and said that history
was bunk. To take this without its context is the height
of ridiculousness, and I am sure that he did not have an
idea of what he was so crudely putting forth.

Although the books have not sold well in this country
and nobody takes Mr. Ford very seriously as a philosopher
(wrongly, in my opinion), Australia sells four or five times
as many as we do here. In England the sale and interest
has also greatly exceeded the same thing in this country.
In Germany I am told that the first volume, translated into
high Deutsch, sold two hundred thousand copies, so that

the new book, *Today and Tomorrow,* was disposed of on the basis of a thousand pounds advance on a ten per cent royalty. Just why these things should happen as they do is more than difficult to unravel.

In addition to the foreign editions that I have mentioned, the *Life* has been translated into almost every civilized language. Thus a prophet is without honor in his own country.

Looking back, it seems strange enough that the Heinemann people had no faith in the [Walter Hines] Page *Letters.* They constantly quoted to me, when I tried to arouse their enthusiasm, the fact that Whitelaw Reid's life had been written and was a dead failure, and Joseph Choate's life had been written and was equally a dead failure, and the English people were not interested in an American ambassador after he had gone home. I remember that the selling department of Heinemann wanted to order five hundred or seven hundred and fifty copies. I would not stand for that, and pressed them successfully to import an edition of two thousand.

As I happened to be in Europe at that time, I arranged for a number of special reviews, and sent early copies to several important journals and writers. Very much to Heinemann's surprise, the newspapers all praised the book extravagantly, and it immediately went out of stock. From that day to this it has sold well, and it has been an interesting and gratifying fact to know that, notwithstanding the jokes on English character cracked by Page, it has been invariably well received.

I think there was only one unfavorable review, and that was in *Blackwood's.* I am reminded of a luncheon party

I attended, when I sat next to the younger Blackwood. He told me that his grandfather, fifty or a hundred years ago, had conceived an intense dislike for America and all things American, and he had made it a rule of the house that nothing favorable to this country should ever be printed in *Blackwood's Magazine.* "So, of course," he said, "we carry out that policy to this day in *Blackwood's."*

Here you have the English prejudice with a vengeance. Young Blackwood personally told me that he had no feeling against the United States, but he regarded the attitude of unfriendliness as a sacred duty.

CHAPTER XXXVIII

THE WINDMILL PRESS

When Charley Evans and his wife were visiting us in the summer of 1925 we motored up to the farm in Manchester, and on the way began to talk of the making of beautiful books. We worked out in more or less detail a scheme for buying a house in England and turning it into a very high type private press. This was not a new scheme, as even at that time there were several presses of this kind, most of them, I think, making a success; but we had several ideas of our own which we thought would do the trick better than anything else, and I think our idea was right.

When we came to talk it over further, it did seem as if perhaps the idea might be developed into a larger enterprise. I had always had in my head a vague and not too definite vision of doing in England what we did in New York and Garden City, but I never brought it up to anybody because there seemed to be so many objections—including the difficulty of interesting the staff itself in the enterprise.

In the fall of 1925 I went to England in the hope of finding a place where we could establish this little press. I had nothing but trouble for five or six weeks and accomplished practically nothing. The first place we found which we thought suitable to our purpose, the real estate agent played us false and we lost the opportunity of purchase. The second place, Banstead, was a beautiful spot and we bought it, paying, I think, about six thousand pounds. It was advertised as an unrestricted freehold, which I thought meant what it said. We had a lawyer examine into the matter, and he reassured us; but we found after we had made the purchase that the local laws prevented the establishment of anything remotely resembling a factory, even if, as in this case, it would employ less than a dozen people. Not wanting to put ourselves in a place where our neighbors would be upset by our presence, we abandoned Banstead, and I think have now sold it, practically getting our money back.

I came home and did not return until the following May, to see a plot which my English partners had found at a place called Kingswood, in Surrey, about fifteen and a half miles from London. I was delighted with the place and much impressed with the possibilities, and after a great deal of trouble, to be sure that it was possible for our press to be erected as a business affair, we purchased the land.

I should go back a bit and tell for a moment how the change in plan came about. We had all accepted the idea of the little Windmill Press, making a few beautiful books and keeping the enterprise down to the most artistic creations we could, without much consideration for the economic side except that the enterprise was to pay for itself and perhaps a little more. We were still discussing this idea when I said one day to Theodore Byard: "Why shouldn't we have a press in England like Country Life Press in the United States?"

I made some investigation and found out from Oliver that our employees, some eighty in number, traveled an average of over two hours and twenty minutes a day from their homes to the office on Bedford Street and back again. This was a waste of time, money, and strength which I thought we could overcome by moving out of town, as we did when we moved to Garden City. I knew that the very idea of the thing would alarm the whole establishment, and so I spoke quite casually of the plan to Theodore, expecting that he would not take it too seriously until the plan had settled a little in his mind and had come up for breath.

I had underestimated my host, because Theodore, with his conscience and sense of responsibility, took the whole subject with immense seriousness. This happened about five o'clock in the afternoon, just after Charley Evans had left the office. About nine o'clock that evening Charley telephoned me from his home, asking if Theodore was ill, because he had been anxious to get him on the telephone but had not been able to do so. I told him that he was all right as far as I knew, but to try to call him up again to make sure.

The next morning both Charley and Theodore approached me with great seriousness. It seemed that I had caused them both a sleepless night. Charley got Theodore on the phone finally, and Theodore told him of this plan, which set them in a quiver of excitement and anxiety.

[241]

Of course, the idea was quite new to Charley, and he said that he did not get to sleep until three o'clock, at which time he made up his mind that probably the plan was all right and there was nothing to worry about.

I feel very proud that within twenty-four hours the idea of the thing was thoroughly understood by Theodore and Charley, and accepted as not only a practical thing to do, but a thing of distinction and untold possibilities. When one considers that this plan has never been worked out by any publishing house in England in all the hundreds of years that have gone by, I think that the staff deserve the greatest credit that they should have caught the idea so quickly and with so much enthusiasm.

This was the start of the larger Windmill Press idea which finally developed at Kingswood, and at this writing a building two hundred feet square and of attractive appearance is being erected.

We found the same trouble with the local Council here that we had met at Banstead, only not quite as virulent; and while I had hoped to close everything up while I was in England in May and June, it took a month or two after I returned before final and full permission was received from the authorities.

One day, being a little weary of these details, which seemed so endless and so annoying, I said to Theodore and Charley: "Perhaps we had better abandon the whole idea."

The response that came to this suggestion made me appreciate how thoroughly and completely the boys had absorbed the idea and how extraordinary was their enthusiasm and their loyalty to the whole plan.

Just how the whole thing will come out is, of course, prophecy. Personally, I am highly enthusiastic and believe that we shall repeat the success of Garden City at Kingswood in a smaller way, as we shall have only something like two hundred employees there against more than a thousand here. In a country like England this plan, if successful, as I believe it will be, will create more attention, even, than our episode in this country. The only three people in England to whom we have talked about it are Galsworthy, who is enthusiastic; Kipling, who approved the vision from the first; and Sir James Barrie, who remarked that there was only one thing against it; namely, that it should have been done by an Englishman instead of an American. All of which cheered me up.*

I want to testify here to the intelligent effort that these good partners of ours have made in investigating every subject which had to do with the creation of this new idea in England.

* A. Dwye Evans, chairman of William Heinemann, Ltd., wrote in 1972:

"Two new wings were opened by W. Somerset Maugham on 24th June 1952. Together they comprise 12,500 square feet.

"Printing and binding activities ceased in 1965 and since that date Kingswood has been devoted to distribution, accounting and promotion activities. [Interestingly, this is true of Doubleday's Garden City location as well.—Ed.] 206 people are employed at Kingswood. As the main distribution centre for Heinemann books, Kingswood warehouses some 5 million books, with a throughput of 7 million copies.

"Plans for the future include a new 20,000 sq. ft. warehouse to be erected to the west of the main building. This has raised architectural questions since it would be impossible today to reproduce the mellowed brick and graceful style of the main building. The intention is to build a modern building of steel and glass which will in no way compete with the main building."

Oliver, who was supposed to be a cashier, soon developed into an expert in building, transportation, printing machinery, and all the points which go to make up so important (to us) an enterprise. Our architect, Lord Gerald Wellesley, was as enthusiastic as could be. Being a son of the Duke of Wellington, he was able to carry a few big guns which had great influence with the powers that be in the County Council. His design is very attractive and his enthusiasm for the work has been unbounded.

Just what the English people will think of it is hard to say, but I have a strong feeling that whether they approve or not at first, when the plan is developed and they see the press, with buildings like an old English college town set in an English park, it will make a great impression. The land is high and has a superb outlook, and consists of about twenty acres. The immediate neighborhood ranging from five to ten miles of Kingswood offers facilities for buying and building houses, so that nobody need live far from his work. This, of course, I regard as a matter of the utmost consequence.

The whole enterprise has been a tremendous pleasure to me, and I have worked over it with great delight when I might have been thinking of less pleasant subjects.†

† Mr. Doubleday wrote later: "If we made any bad mistakes, I have not heard about them; very satisfactory progress has been made from the beginning. One trouble we had which was bound to come; namely, our proofreading was not too good; but we have had the same kind of trouble in Garden City, and every printing house in Christendom that I know anything about has, I think, difficulty in its proof room first, last, and all the time. . . .

"I am reminded of an experience which George Mifflin, of Houghton Mifflin Company, once told me. They were supposed to have the best proof room in the country. They had made a set of books for some Harvard University professors. The proofs had been read by all twelve authors of the books and were said to be letter-perfect. The chief editor was so pleased with the enterprise that he had a paragraph printed in the first volume in which he gave credit for the excellent proofreading to the various people concerned . . . when the books were delivered the word 'proof' had been spelled 'poof.' "

CHAPTER XXXIX

SOME ENGLISH FRIENDS

LORD NORTHCLIFFE

ONE of my best friends, with whom I had many delightful experiences, was Lord Northcliffe, whom I knew twenty-five years ago as Alfred Harcourt. If I should attempt to tell all the adventures that I had with him, it would take me forever. He visited us in Oyster Bay, and in this way I came to know him well. I enjoyed our talks tremendously; as a matter of fact, they were more like monologues, because he always had so much to say that I was delighted to keep still, look, and listen. His mind worked so rapidly and with such precision and vigor that I confess after three or four hours of it I was extremely exhausted trying to keep up with him. Such activity and stress as he carried day in and day out could hardly fail to have its effect on him; I presume he died from a worn-out brain.

Every Christmas he used to send me a telegram, and he did countless little things which endeared him to me very much. Among other presents was a jade cigar box. He had two of them, and he said, "Now I shall give you one and have your name put with mine," his initials having already been engraved on the jade. But he could find no one in London who could put the initials on the stone without the chance of breaking the box, so my box had his crest and initials alone. But it was a beautiful gift. I remember he brought it to me at Brown's Hotel one time when American Ambassador John W. Davis was having tea with us. He had never met Northcliffe, and they had a long discussion about political matters far over my head.

When we arrived in England in December 1918, it was impossible most of the time to get even a taxi, and gasoline was worth its weight in gold. Northcliffe put his car at our disposal, because he said he was going to France and would be glad to have us use it. It was certainly a great help and convenience.

I always thought that Northcliffe expected to be made one of the English commissioners to settle the peace; in fact, I am sure he expected it. He had some trouble with Lloyd George, and at the last moment Northcliffe's name was dropped and someone else was substituted. This, I think, was a deep disappointment to Alfred, and he went away to the south of France and stayed during the first few weeks of the conference.

I was visiting once in a London club which had a bust of Napoleon at the top of the stairs. I had been invited there to tea by a very stodgy old Englishman, and as we were going up these marble stairs with the white marble bust of Napoleon and the beehive before us, I remarked, for want of something to say:

"That, I presume, is Northcliffe and his busy little bees."

He stopped me with a look of horror and said: "No, that isn't Northcliffe; that is Napoleon."

Not being able to think of anything to say, I carried on in humiliation.

One day at Brown's Hotel, Kipling, Northcliffe, and American Ambassador Davis came to tea—three most interesting people who talked about the most interesting things. I did an unusual thing with Rud and asked him if he would not repeat the verses about Ed Baker, the poem begun twenty-five years ago and just completed. Much to my surprise he did so, and Northcliffe and Davis were duly impressed.

A week later we dined alone with the Davises at the American Embassy. Davis expressed his interest and appreciation in having been allowed to meet Kipling and to hear these verses.

I said, "I have heard them at least a dozen times. I only wish I could remember them."

"I can remember what they were," he replied, and he repeated most of the poem, having heard it only once. I thought it an extraordinary feat of memory.

In Nassau last winter I spoke to him about it again, and he again repeated the poem, showing, I think, the most retentive memory I have ever met in my life.

SIR JAMES BARRIE

One has curious experiences sometimes, and not always easy ones to meet.

I knew Mr. and Mrs. Barrie very well, but never got along with Mrs. Barrie and was not particularly interested in her. After she left her husband I was disgusted with her, and my opinion fell to a low ebb.

One time later, I was visiting Willie Meredith, son of George Meredith, at his home, and was invited to meet a lady whom he said I knew, though he did not tell me who she was. I was dressed earlier than any of the rest of the people in the house, and came down to the drawing room only to find myself face to face with Mrs. Barrie and the pimply-faced poet she had married. I was thrown into a perfect funk, but the former Mrs. Barrie came forward most cheerfully and cordially and said that she was so glad to see me again and added, "Do you know who I am?"

I knew darned well who she was, but I could not think of anything to say, so I said that I had many friends in England and often got confused, not seeing them for long periods at a time.

"I used to be Mrs. Barrie," she said, "and you have been entertained at my house many times."

I was covered with confusion and could think of nothing further to say. Meanwhile, the nondescript husband stood by looking like a sheep. I was almost in a state of nervous collapse when Meredith came down and the situation was somewhat relieved.

Barrie was very good to his wife and I do not think he ever recovered from the shock and the stress that the whole business caused him. I saw him in London in 1926 and had a delightful time with him. He had written a play, *Shall We Join the Ladies?* or rather, had written one act of such a play, but it had never been completed and he says never will be completed, as he has lost interest in the whole subject. Apparently he has been asked one hundred and fifty thousand times about the other two acts, but he still refuses to give any hint of what he was going to do with the complete work. In my humble judgment, he did not and does not know himself.

An example of English reserve occurred in connection with Barrie and Frere Reeves. Frere was at our hotel when we gave our luncheon to Barrie, and he saw the author for two or three hours on end. Three or four days after that he was at a moving picture show, and he noticed next door to him a little man smoking a pipe. He came gradually to realize that his seat mate was Sir James Barrie. Under ordinary circumstances you would expect that they would immediately speak, as both were alone and there were several lapses in the moving picture; but Frere Reeves did not speak to Barrie and Barrie did not speak to Frere, and at the end of the evening they went their ways without a word. I took Frere to task for this, and he said it would have been undignified for him to have forced his personality on Sir James—a queer idea from my point of view.

Speaking of the play, *Shall We Join the Ladies?*—Barrie gave permission for the production of the completed act to some charity, and among the audience was the Prince of Wales. As the curtain rang down the house was absolutely silent, and Barrie heard the Prince say to his aide: "That's that. What damn thing do we have to go to next?"—which Barrie thought was a very good comment on the performance.

I have known Barrie for twenty-five years, and he has always been friendly and interested and altogether delightful. Seeing so much of him this last time I was in Europe was a great pleasure, as for years our paths had not crossed. In one respect he has changed a good deal from the old days. He was the most silent man I ever knew— I think that the President [Coolidge] is a chatterbox in comparison—but when he was with us at our hotel last June he talked like a magpie and told story after story, Scotch, English, and American, and was in every way most delightful and even more charming than in the old days.

He spoke of our moving Heinemann to the country and said that he entirely disapproved of it. I was rather distressed at this, as I took him seriously, and asked him why.

"Some English publisher should have done it first," he said; "it is humiliating to have an American come over and do this obvious and necessary thing."

He has adopted a young man named Peter Davies, who has also become a publisher and who talked to me much about our plant moving to Kingswood. He felt the same as his uncle, and expressed himself most forcibly.

VISCOUNT GREY

Not very long after Lord Grey resigned his position as Minister of Foreign Affairs, I received an invitation from him to make him a little visit in London, which, of course, I was glad to accept. I had met him formally two or three times, but had had no opportunity to talk with him, so this invitation gave me genuine pleasure.

He came into the room groping from chair to chair, his eyesight was so bad; he took my hand most cordially and with such a nice spirit, and said: "Could you be Effendi, of whom I have heard Mr. Page talk so much?"

I certainly felt deeply flattered, and we had a long talk in which he told me many things about Page and his ambitions, and his own troubles in the way of his physical condition, which was very bad at the time but which was notably improving.

One of the most miserable mistakes that we ever made was in declining to pay five thousand pounds advance on his book. I blame myself for having been a pusillanimous clam, and I have several excuses that I could think of, but none of them are worth setting down here, because there is no excuse for giving up a really fine book like this because it might mean a small loss of money. This is one of the worst book mistakes we ever made, and I trust that I shall never make another one like it; but if it had to go to anybody outside of our shop, I am glad that it went to Stokes,* who is a good fellow and needs good books even more, perhaps, than we do.

* Frederick A. Stokes (1857–1939) had his own firm, Frederick A. Stokes Company.

CHAPTER XL

THE STRANGE CHARACTER
OF COLONEL LAWRENCE

AT THE BEGINNING of 1919, when [a group of] American journalists were visiting England, they gave a big dinner at one of the hotels—the usual formal sort of affair which to most people is a great bore. I had been kindly invited by somebody whom I now forget, but I think it was Evelyn Wrench. My next-door neighbor was a young-looking man of, I should say, not more than twenty-seven or twenty-eight, who talked with extraordinary brilliancy and with whom I struck up quite a friendship, as one sometimes does on such occasions, but not very often with an Englishman.

When the dinner was over and we came to part, we shook hands and I said that it was a misfortune for me that our paths would part and I very likely should not see him again, but I should remember with the greatest pleasure this evening which we had spent together.

He said, "Why shouldn't we see each other again?" And I told him that I was in London for only two or three weeks; that my name was Doubleday; I was a publisher and was staying at Brown's Hotel; and if he would come to dinner, I should much enjoy it.

He said that his name was Lawrence and he would come with pleasure, and the date was fixed. At that particular moment he was one of the most famous men in England: he was Colonel Lawrence of Mesopotamian and Arabian fame and was a conspicuous influence. Lowell Thomas was giving a lecture on his adventures which was filling Covent Garden every night. All this, I am sorry to say, I did not dream of, and the name Lawrence meant nothing to me.

I spoke to Kipling about him the next day and described his appearance, and Kipling said: "He is one of the most interesting characters, if not the most interesting, that came out of the war, and I should be glad to come to your little dinner and meet him if you would like to have me"—which, of course, from my point of view was highly desirable.

Somehow we got mixed up on our dates, and Lawrence appeared about half past eight the next night. Florence and I were dining alone that particular evening, and were much surprised to see Lawrence walking in. We straightened out the fact that we were wrong on dates, and he asked if he might stay to dinner that night which, of course, we were delighted to have him do. Thus we came to know him better.

Colonel Thomas Lawrence, whom all the world knows, is a mysterious person, a queer individuality, and perhaps the most interesting as well as the strangest that I have ever met. Before we had finished our first night's meeting at Brown's Hotel, I had come to feel that I knew him intimately, and by persistent effort had wormed out of him a lot of his stories of his experiences of blowing up German trains, the organization of the Arabs, and all sorts of weird and extraordinary tales.

The next night he came again, and Kipling and Alan Bott were there, and I never heard more brilliant conversation. This was the beginning of quite a friendship with Tom Lawrence. When we came home he wrote me letters and we had a correspondence that lasted for a couple of years.

A delightful experience with Lawrence occurred when we went to Paris at the beginning of 1919 when the Peace Conference was on. Lawrence was there with Feisal,* who represented the Arabs. He introduced Mrs. Doubleday and me to Feisal, who invited us to dinner, which was considered a great honor, as it was said to be the first time that he had invited a lady as his guest.

Feisal came, also, to take tea with us in his gorgeous robes. Lawrence, too, was dressed up as an Arab chief. They certainly made a picturesque appearance in Paris, not so conspicuous as they would have been at other times, because the whole city was full of people in costume attending the Peace Conference.

I was very anxious to get Lawrence to write something for *The World's Work,* which he did, and handed it to me. I told him that it was very good, but suggested that he should add to it and make it a little longer. He said that he would do this and took it away with him. When next

* He would become King of Iraq in 1921.

I saw him he told me that he thought it was no good and he had destroyed it. He also had written a large portion of the manuscript of his book, which he either destroyed or lost.

We saw a good deal of him in Paris and he made our visit very enjoyable. Later on he entertained Nelson and Patty, and Dorothy and Huntington [Babcock], and showed the most friendly interest in everything that concerned us. But I am convinced that authors are not the only strange people in the world. Sometimes soldiers and diplomats are a bit queer. Certainly Lawrence fulfilled this description.

He had the most peculiar notions about the publication of his book. First he was going to have one copy printed and put in the British Museum, and he made a dozen different plans. I told him that I was more interested in the book because of our association together than as a publishing enterprise, and finally we worked out a plan which provided for our copyrighting the volume in his name and safeguarding his control. I never dreamed that things would turn out as they did. A young literary agent named Savage came to me and said that Lawrence had put his book into his (Savage's) hands. I asked Lawrence about this, and he said that it was untrue; that he had not put his book in anybody's hands, but controlled it himself, and when it came to be made I was the one to do it. We had even talked about the format, the type to be used, etc.

What was my astonishment in 1925 to be told by Doran that he had secured the publication rights of this book through Savage. The mystery has never been cleared up and I cannot understand yet just what happened. The last

I heard, the book was to be sold for ten thousand dollars a copy, or some absurd amount of money like that.†

I presume the story will ultimately be explained if the book is ever published, which I doubt. Lawrence sent me seven chapters which, so far as I know, are the only ones in existence not in his own possession.

I was a good deal embarrassed by gifts of books which he continually sent me, and felt that our friendship was a thing of lasting value. Apparently he is the most erratic person on earth. The last I heard of him he had gone back to the Air Force as a private under the name of Shaw, having had the distinguished position of British colonel, with every kind of medal and honor, offered to him, none of which would he accept.

When we went to England he always met us, and we visited him in Oxford, as he did us at Brown's Hotel. The story is not ended, but as far as it has gone it is certainly inexplicable. I hope to live to understand what really happened.

[Mr. Doubleday wrote later, in a recollection called "Friendships"]:

Seven years flew over my head before I saw Lawrence again (I think it was seven years—anyhow, it was a long time). During these years I occasionally received a letter from him and wrote one in reply, and we had some studies together about the making of fine books, in which he is an adept and a collector as well.

† This was *The Seven Pillars of Wisdom*. A limited number of copies was offered for sale by George H. Doran Company in 1926. Doubleday, Doran & Company published a slightly revised version in 1935.

In 1929 the Soviets claimed that he was acting as a British spy in Afghanistan. There was no truth in this, as he was stationed in a small Indian village, a member of the Air Force, but for the sake of peace and quiet life the British government, as I understand it, undertook to bring him home. . . . I received a letter from him, saying that he was in Plymouth and asking if we could not stop off on our way from New York to London to see him.

For some reason this turned out not to be convenient, and on the spur of the moment I sent him a telegram asking if he could not meet me in London, to which he replied in the affirmative. After some further telegraphic correspondence he agreed to motorcycle up from Plymouth one Saturday afternoon and stay with us until Sunday, a period of twenty-four hours.

He has an old motorcycle, and he left Plymouth about one o'clock Saturday afternoon, arriving at our house in Hyde Park Terrace at five minutes past seven o'clock the same evening, keeping his appointment to the minute.

Meanwhile, I had telegraphed Kipling asking if I could bring Lawrence with me to Burwash, Sunday, provided the weather was suitable. A quick response came from Kipling, saying to bring Lawrence anyhow, whether the weather was suitable or not. Lawrence telegraphed to his commander and got his leave extended until Monday morning, with the understanding that he would be back in quarters before eight o'clock.

We had a glorious time. Saturday evening we spent three or four hours in renewing our youth, since he had just achieved his fortieth birthday. We talked until Mrs.

Doubleday made us go to bed and resumed early the next morning.

On Sunday we spent the afternoon with Rud and Carrie in another flood of talk. I sat on the sidelines and listened to Kipling and Lawrence dissect the universe and put it together again.

We arrived back at Hyde Park Terrace in time for dinner, and at ten o'clock he wheeled out his motorcycle and started for Plymouth, a run of two hundred and sixty miles. I felt very guilty to have put him to the trouble of traveling more than five hundred miles to make a visit to an old friend, but he appears to have enjoyed his experience very much. He certainly leads the simple life.

One of the most graceful letters that I ever received in my life was his bread and butter note, which I copy here, as these memoirs are secret, just for the sake of the record:

Plymouth

28 . VI . 29

Effendim:

I have done ten days solid duty in camp, and am again free to go out: only instead of that I write you a line, to recall that very golden day we had. Do you know, it was all exquisite? Kingswood, Kipling, Knole, Ashdown Forest, the lunch. Years since I drove, lordly, in a pleasure car: the R.A.F. has its transport, of course, but that is hardly driving. The leisure of our progress along the roads, and the warmth and good talk inside the car all left a happy feeling. It was a great, exceptional day: and as it gets more distant I perceive my debt to you an increasing one. You is plural. Mrs. Doubleday at last

[259]

loses the distinction of a postscript. She made half the pleasure of that trip. I hope that you and she also still enjoy it. Of course it isn't so rare a pleasure, for you. You (and she) would have to join the Air Force to squeeze all the flavour out of luxury. Only when one person is as happy as I was, the other two must have felt some sunshine.

The R.A.F. here appears to value my services. At least I work all day at its jobs. Just I have half an hour in the morning, before breakfast, which I keep for my own reading. I make the half-hour, by getting up before reveille. One can't read in odd half-hours: reading is to soak oneself hour after hour all day in a single real book, until the book is realler than one's chair or world: but I've done most of the Brook Kerith in these half-hours: and tasted the Heinemann life (only half-kind to him, that book is. It feels as though the poor little man hadn't been properly understood) and read all Enid Bagnold's Happy Foreigner. That last is surprisingly distinguished. I give her full marks for a good book.

Frere Reeves wrote to me, two excellent letters, about good printing. I shall go to see him when, or if, I get leave in October. I have a design of sliding down some odd day (Dear, it will be an odd day!) if he permits it, and I achieve it, with Bernard Shaw & Mrs. Shaw. She is quaint & comfortable, and fresh, & kind. G.B.S. is exciting, per contra. Together they are like bacon and eggs, a harmony in blue and silver. I fear I talk nonsense.

Do go on writing your memoirs. Put in that story about the roses pinned to the pickets. Dictate quite a lot, for then that dry sparkle will cling to the words. Pens are stiff things to hold, and they make our words too mannered.

Not to spoil the pleasure ship with work I put a

business request on a spare sheet. Remember me very much to Mrs. Doubleday. Tell her to start imagining another excursion for next time. If it's only 1/10 as good as that it'll be good enough.

Yours ever,

T. E. Shaw

I've had twinges of conscience, since, that perhaps I tempted you to overdo things that day. I am so indecently fit and durable. I hope you were not ill or tired, even.

Among other things, we asked Lawrence why he changed his name to Shaw. He said that he wanted to make a new deal with life when he returned from the East, so he decided to adopt a new English name. His method of doing this was rather characteristic. He took a telephone book and decided that he would pick the first name containing only four letters at the top of the first left-hand page. This turned out to be S-h-a-w, and he appears to have adopted this name for good.

Being a private, he had to wear his uniform, and I must say that he looked very handsome and about twice as strong physically as he was when I saw him last.

On our way to the Kiplings' we stopped at Kingswood and his enthusiasm for the press was a great help to me. He accepted our ideas as practical, and it was great fun to prophesy what would happen. It may not all happen, but we had the pleasure of prophesying—which is a good thing to have in the house and is not too expensive.

Since the above was written much water has run over the dam. Lawrence is still on his job in India, working as a regular soldier for, I think, about two pounds a week. I have constant letters from him on literary subjects, and he divulges very little about himself. After all, although he sold his book to Doran, it is now a part of the Garden City outfit.

I think Lawrence's career may be watched with much interest. As I have already said, he goes under the name of Shaw and apparently has entirely dropped the name of Lawrence. He was a natural son, and he wrote me that one name was as good as another. I have a genuine affection for him, and the time may come when he will make a great figure in the Far East or India.

Copy of [a] letter recently received follows:

Effendim:

I have to use pencil to-day, for I'm sitting in the shop watching that some workmen don't steal our bits lying about; and writing on my knee. It will be worse written than usual, I fear.

About Effendi. That's a Turkish title, meaning a Lord or leader: and it is used too freely in Turkey, as Esq. is dabbed after the name of every Englishman who can read and write.

So the Turks found that it would be more ceremonious to say Effendim: the plural: meaning Lords or Leaders or Sirs. And a Turk who's talking to his better will say always "Effendim" to him. Like the French "Tu" the singular has grown too free and easy.

Kipling of course can "Tutoyer" you. He is one of the very big things. "Effendim" comes from me with a better grace.

"Effendina" it was once. That's royal. I used to call Abdul Hamid, the Sultan of Turkey, "Effendina." I tried to call you "Effendina": but after two or three tries it fell flat & Effendim came in. I think it may be a by-blow of the absurd fancy we cherish in England that America somehow is a sort of Republic: everybody free & equal, and Kings and Queens felt to be flyblown ornaments. You will laugh to hear my Victorian ideas.

So Kipling is quite right: and I am quite right, one step below him. Effendi from me to you would be presumption.

T.E.S.

CHAPTER XLI

A PHILOSOPHY
OF PUBLISHING

I SHOULD be grateful if I could write anything which would be valuable on the philosophy of the publishing business, especially if it would help the coming generation to clear up some spots which are not too easily understood. I have devoted a good part of my life to trying to formulate some philosophy to guide me in our enterprises. Some of these things are very clear in my own mind and I hope I shall not be accused of too much dogmatism if I set them down here.

I have tried to work out a formula which would help me and which I hope might help others to acquire a broader mental attitude, and have endeavored to state in a few words the salient features of what success means from my point of view. For a long time I have carried these few phrases around with me, feeling that they would be a guide and inspiration at least to myself. The expression of my sentiment reads as follows:

A Hope!

That we should be clever enough to make sufficient profit to permit us to treat with a wise generosity all employees, customers, and those from whom we buy!

The publishing business in many respects resembles every other commercial enterprise, but it differs in at least one aspect. I remember that Lord Northcliffe put his finger on the truth when he said, "You are in a business which requires re-creation every year, and sometimes twice a year."

This may have a substantial merit, in that a publishing business cannot go very wrong without becoming moribund or inflicted with dry rot, because month by month and year by year it has to be practically remade, only a small portion of last year's books being good for this year.

Personally, I am very much impressed with the difficulty of expanding a publishing business and at the same time upholding and advancing its character and quality, without which its moral influence has very little value. I think, too, that we often fail to realize the enormous responsibility that Doubleday, Page & Company has. I hope and believe that none of our product will do harm, but whether we avail ourselves of our opportunities to do good by publishing only worthy books and issuing many of them, is a grave question; in fact, I know that we do not. We come, then, to the subject of what is good and healthful, and what is puerile and useless writing. To keep the true balance between the useful and the useless is a man's job.

I have often thought, also, that in our eagerness to expand the business we increase the overhead in such a way that it acts as a perpetual and possibly a vicious circle. This year you do so much business; next year you do so much more business; but unless you stretch every nerve, you make no more money and have no more substantial property than when you proceeded on a more moderate scale, and you are involved with obligations for the coming year most difficult to meet. In order to face this increased demand, the temptation is strong to do foolish things in a hectic chase after more sales. One is inclined, I think, to break down one's morale in discounts, overselling, and other undesirable things. This is particularly so in a large concern, and its influence is most subtle and to my mind really injurious. I can recall many instances when, in order to get a large sale, perhaps for a particular month, we have committed what we all thought, when we came to judge it soberly, was an unwise action.

I suppose I am likely to be accused of being old-fashioned, but I insist upon it that I am not. I think it should be the new fashion, rather, to build up quality instead of the more obvious and easy achievement of building up quantity, and I believe it will be. There are many who appreciate quantity, but who fail to appreciate the real value of a better output.

There arises in connection with this subject our early experience when we started Doubleday, Page & Company. I can remember as if it were yesterday Mr. and Mrs. Page and Nellie and myself discussing together the prospects of the new enterprise. First in our consideration was the quality of the books we were to publish. We made the vow that we would not permit Doubleday, Page & Company's imprint ever to go on a book that would do harm,

or that we should be ashamed of. As I look back over
the years, I wish our record were a little better than it is,
although I think we have resisted opportunities to make
money on unworthy books as often as most publishers,
and perhaps more often. Unnumbered times we have been
tempted to take up the type of book which a certain class
of new publishing house finds successful and congenial,
and I hope we have managed to avoid these pitfalls. As
time goes on, the temptation is going to be greater and
greater. In the first place, we have got this increasing overhead, which requires that we do everything to gain sales.
Also, there is the feeling of laxity which comes over an organization which does not think of this subject as seriously
as it should be considered. I do hope that as the years go
by our list will be finer. For selfish interests alone, this
is a wise thing to bring about, because immoral or unworthy books do not pay, and destroy the very fiber of a
business organization. I wish everybody in the shop felt
this as strongly as Mr. and Mrs. Page and Nellie did
twenty-five years ago. I still feel the obligation that those
dear people laid upon us, and I pass it along to my
successors.

I have spoken very often of our ideas and experiences,
with little mention of my partners, who worked hand in
glove with me. As I look back on it, one of the greatest
reasons for our success was that we worked absolutely
together. For years we had a saying that anybody who was
in a minority had his leg chopped off. This was true, and
so far as I am concerned, I do not think that I insisted
upon doing anything with which most of my partners
disagreed. In telling all these stories, I have failed to

mention which of my partners were concerned with me, but we worked so closely that the matter of credit was not much of an affair between us. It was not a question of who invented a scheme—we all carried it through to success. This happened regularly year after year. On the shade of the lamp on my desk in the office is pasted a paragraph which I cut from a Southern Negro newspaper. It reads: *You can do a lot of good in the world if you don't care who gets the credit for it.*

It is beyond me to write of the vision I have always had at the base of my brain of the extent to which a publishing business could be carried in moral influence as well as in volume. Its power for good is enormous, and I believe that even yet half the tale is not told of what will eventually prove to be a great publishing enterprise, covering all departments and covering them in new ways. Certainly we have not begun to achieve our maximum sales. We shall learn year by year to add to our customers in a way that we as yet hardly appreciate. Then will come the selection of books, which will be not merely for the purpose of sale, but for the purpose of influence as well.

As a dim possibility which would require much effort and skill to work out, a thing like this might happen in the idealistic publishing enterprise about which I am talking. My friend, Dr. Frederick Tilney, told me a day or two ago of a great Russian physician seventy-odd years old who has made some of the greatest contributions to the science of medicine. He has recently written a book, or a series of articles or letters, with the basic argument that civilization is not yet able to use its brain as it should be used. Dr. Tilney said he believes that in all the centuries of man's existence, perhaps five hundred thousand years, we have only developed the brain to about one fifth of its possible capacity. This Russian scientist, who was so great a man that even the Bolsheviks respected him and left him alone to go on with his work, has, Dr. Tilney told me, developed a statement of what should be done by the present generation to cultivate the human brain and make the world better, and help every person to help himself to achieve the best that his intellectual fiber can create.

Suppose that such a book as this should be written and put in convenient and popular form: the methods which we have used on the Pocket University could be applied to the sale of a book like this, and its success would contribute tremendously to the world. I am going to ask Dr. Tilney to develop this idea and talk to our people about it. If one could go into enterprises like this with a feeling of power and success brought about by our clever or able methods, we would have an institution which the next generation would be proud of. Isn't it possible! We have to have some dreams to live on to keep us cheered up.

Recently I looked over the list of publications of Doubleday, Page & Company beginning in 1897, the very start of our business. It may be my imagination, but I really believe that, largely because of small capital, the books were selected with unusual skill for immediate and lasting success. For instance, in the first two years of our publishing life we issued books by Rudyard Kipling, Mark Twain, Conan Doyle, Stephen Crane, Mary E. Wilkins, Frank Norris, Henry George, etc., also *Bird Neighbors,* by Neltje Blanchan, which was an immense success at once.

As I remember these early enterprises, we had to make

each book pay for itself as promptly as possible and go on selling year after year. One of the most notable instances of this was the series of small books called Little Master-pieces, sold in cloth, if I remember rightly, for thirty cents a volume, and set up and printed by De Vinne in his best style. Several of these were published in our first autumn season, and new volumes were added through the years. I would not dare to say how many million volumes have been sold; we know that the Pocket University, which is practically a new edition of the Little Masterpieces, has not only had a tremendous sale but has had an influence of a good kind.

Another set, the Law Library, which I had tried to get Scribner to take up, the young firm made. I think we must have published and sold at least four or five million volumes, and it is sold in ten-thousand lots even to this day.

A good bank balance is inclined to make one careless in the selection of books, but this is a subject so easy to argue and so difficult to prove that it is hardly worth writing about. I feel very strongly, and in principle I think all the staff agree with me, that every time we put on our list a book which is unworthy and does not come up to our standard it injures our business in the eyes of the booksellers. Except in *special* instances, a volume which sells less than two or three thousand copies is usually a liability and drags down our average, and puts unsalable volumes on the shelves of the booksellers, which is a real source of injury assuming that the book has not a special market, or does not advance a good cause, or for some other reason should not be included in this class—I do not wish to give the idea that the matter of quantity should be the controlling factor.

A point which I think deserves more attention than it is apt to get is the duplication of books on a single subject. I have often seen a publisher accept and issue a volume which is almost an exact duplicate of a book on the same subject and of the same character which may have been issued successfully or unsuccessfully months or years before. This leads to a vast duplication of titles which are not sufficiently better or different to justify their publication. Take, for instance, the garden books. There are two or three volumes on every detail of gardening, so that the whole garden interest is covered several times over. This is a subject, as I have said before, which is worthy of more attention than is likely to be given to it.

The one quality which I think is lacking in most publishing houses, and, indeed, in all new business enterprises, is courage. It is so much easier to follow in the footsteps of those who have preceded, and so difficult to mark out new paths and tread them with the head up and the eye clear on the future.

When we moved to Garden City we, of course, took a great risk; but we all had in mind that if we could make the success that we thought we could, we might be of benefit to the whole publishing trade and induce others to follow our example, always, as I have said, provided we succeeded in a large way. We have succeeded, and I like to think and feel that a thousand people do not travel in the subway, but have good light, comfortable and healthful surroundings, good pay, and are not obliged to spend long hours in traveling back and forth.

I have always believed that when a firm reaches the place where it might consider itself an institution it should control its own output. I mean by this that it should not have to combine with other publishers to save expense. The same thing is true of manufacturing. We have a capacity in our place to make a very large number of books daily. We should, and I hope will, ultimately have a capacity to sell an equally large number of books daily without having to go outside to get printing work.*

Another point of the utmost importance is that this work done by our own press should be in every way equal to and, indeed, superior to the same work done by other presses; and this should be easily possible because we control the matter contributed to the press and the manner of its execution.

Still another point which is hard to work out, especially as the concern reaches larger proportions, is to keep one's staff quick to see merit and courageous to follow it out. The more money one makes, the more difficult it is to do this. Because we work at Garden City in harmony, I feel that its co-operative influence will grow as time goes on, and pride in the organization should far outweigh any pride in individual credit.

Speaking of courage—I have been amused, if not distressed, to watch over a series of years the lack of courage in sending out magazines for sale. In the case of almost every individual I have ever known who had the authority

* Today, in the 1970s, our book manufacturing facilities are used exclusively for books which are published by the Doubleday Publishing Company or sold by other divisions or subsidiaries of Doubleday & Company, Inc.—Ed.

to do so, a greater number of magazines has been distributed than there was any reasonable expectation of selling. This has always rather surprised me, as I never could see any particular delight in throwing away ink and paper. I hope the time will come when we shall have the courage to lose a few sales, if necessary, and keep the supply within reasonable limits of return. It is not only saving expense, but the influence of this courageous action goes promptly back to the editorial managers of the magazine and the merit of its literary contents. This, I think, is of even more importance than saving money on returns. The essence of the whole matter is that small returns mean a good magazine, and large returns mean a poor magazine.

I presume this situation is not strange when one remembers that for thirty or forty years the American News Company has taught its clients that large returns are a necessity and should be accepted in any quantity. I do hope we have reached the point where we have the courage to face the common sense of this situation.

CHAPTER XLII

STAFF MEETINGS

I HAVE often wondered of just how much value the system of running a business by meetings of the staff is. Since it has been our method for twenty-five years and we have not lost money for a single year during these two decades which have passed over our heads, it would seem that we have proved the success of the plan. The chartered accountants tell me that this record is remarkable, and I pay a tribute to the staff when I say that I believe hardly any other publishing house in the country has had the same experience.

But looking back on it, there seem to me very many opportunities for making these meetings more useful. Perhaps the one which has distributed the most money out of the treasury is the Net Results Club—the sum given away in net results bonuses during the last twenty-five years must have aggregated several hundred thousand dollars. I think in the beginning this organization was very valuable, as it served to educate its members in the workings of departments outside of their own. I fear, however, that its usefulness has gradually become less as the novelty of the meetings has worn off. The only way to make such a plan valuable year after year is to prepare a program which stimulates and interests each member. This can be done in either one or two ways: the chairman can dominate the meeting and bring up interesting and important features, or the members themselves can do the stimulating. It is years since I have attended a Net Results meeting and I am not very competent to speak of just what goes on; but I can remember well the extraordinary effort that I used to have to make to think up plans to talk of which would inspire the Net Results group and carry the meetings through to success. Certainly, it would be valuable if we could make some change which would put vital force into this affair. Running over a quarter of a century, it is bound to become more or less stale, like the remittance man who receives from his family his check for the first month when he is away from home and responds with enthusiastic thanks; the second check brings less thanks; the third still less; and in the case of the fourth he kicks like thunder because the check is a day late. So it is with an organization like the Net Results.

Just recently Nelson has taken up the study of this Club and worked out subjects which I understand from various sources have aroused the utmost interest from the members. He is doing exactly what I hoped he could do when he took this job in hand, and I am sure the yield, directly or indirectly, will be very large and very useful, not only to the company, but to the members as well, since I believe it greatly broadens their interest and increases their efficiency.

As to the Magazine, the Budget, and the Book Meetings —I think they are very valuable, but here again the meeting is more valuable the better it is organized: either the chairman must make a study before the meeting is convened, and dominate it and carry it through with some enthusiasm, or the spirit and vision must come through the members themselves, which is almost impossible to achieve. One trouble is that there are likely to be too many in the room, and the timid ones are too shy to talk and give forth their opinions, either positive or negative. I think that this is a subject which we can well study, a thing really of the utmost importance, and something new might accomplish great results, particularly if fundamental subjects are taken up and studied.

I am glad to hear from London that this examination of the value of meetings is being taken up by the staff there. They have the same general troubles in London that we have in Garden City, but the plan should be more interesting, because they have not been cut and dried for so many years: we have too many traditions to meet in Garden City, whereas I feel that the Heinemann meetings will be more fruitful of results, because so many things which are old stories to us are only now being developed there. Perhaps by some good fortune we shall be able to find ways of accomplishing some things along new lines.

CHAPTER XLIII

THE DIFFICULT ART
OF SELLING BOOKS

Of course, books may be sold in many ways, but we have been fortunate enough to have four distinct departments to try to sell the largest quantity by these various means. There is the trade—that is, the bookseller; there is mail-order selling; there is the book contract department; and there is the subscription book wholesale department which deals with general agents. I presume as time goes on the methods of selling will increase in number and certainly in efficiency.

To begin first with the trade department: I am inclined to think that this is the least developed, which is natural, because we can only approach our customer through the cumbersome method of selling the book to the dealer, and by some good luck or advertising move the book from his shelves into the possession of the purchaser. The troublesome thing in this connection is the fact that one can prove almost anything for or against. I can prove, for example, from definite quoted experiences, that advertising pays, and I can prove beyond question that it does not pay. I can prove that it pays to treat the trade in certain ways, and that it does not pay to treat the trade in certain ways. So at best it is only a rough rule-of-thumb calculation.

Perhaps the most difficult of all our problems is how much we shall spend for advertising. Human nature likes to see its name in print, and the temptation to advertise is overpowering, particularly when one cannot prove that it does not pay. And the author demands a lot of advertising, and the bookseller expects it, though he does not accept responsibility in helping us to get our money back.

I do not know in what direction the book trade will develop, but to date, looking back over my experience of twenty-five or thirty years, the increase of stores and of volume has been and is disappointing. Just at the present time there are more shops being established, and I think more booksellers making money; but this does not mean that there is any increased activity in new ideas, or any special vision shown by the people engaged in the delightful business of spreading good books about the world.

For many years there has been no new invention that I know of for selling books in a different way, until the Book-of-the-Month Club came along just a few months ago. We have been fortunate in having four books chosen by the committee out of the seven which they have so far recommended. The order for the last one, Ellen Glasgow's novel, *The Romantic Comedians,* was thirty-five thousand copies, and I suppose it is quite possible that the number of subscribers may run to one hundred thousand. Here we have a totally original idea, so far as I know, made possible by the fact that the people who select the books

[278]

are favorably known to a large class of readers who believe that these selections are honestly made. Certainly, a year ago we never dreamed of such a development. Perhaps other things will come along as unusual and as successful as this: certainly, this has been a great achievement for the deviser of the scheme and a valuable thing for us, though we can hardly expect to keep up our record of having more than fifty per cent of the selections.

The mail-order department, which in our case has assumed large proportions and to which Nelson has devoted much of his time, has the merit of working on a scientific basis. If Nelson spends a thousand dollars on advertising, he knows approximately how nearly the advertising pays, and he can cut it out or alter it or repeat it, just as the figures indicate. To me the possibilities of the mail-order business seem greater for this reason than the possibilities of the trade. To begin with, the dealer gets about forty per cent off, and this is supposed to pay him for special activity in selling our books. But he does not really, except in rare cases, sell the books at all—he simply supplies them; but forty per cent expense in advertising for the mail-order department nearly pays the whole expense of securing the order and actually reaches the customer.

Take, for example, the case of the *Book of Etiquette*. This was published twenty or twenty-five years ago and was regarded as a successful publication; it sold possibly ten thousand copies in ten or fifteen years. Nelson comes along with a new idea—"What's wrong with this picture," etc.*—and sells a million copies at a higher price than the trade edition. The booksellers are stimulated by this

* The sort of advertising headline used in the mail-order ads.

[279]

advertising, and they also sell more copies than they ever did before. This is an example of what can be done with an old book if it is cleverly marketed and put forth to reach a large number of buyers. There is no limit, as I look at it, to what may happen with the mail-order business if we can develop it along interesting and original lines.

Then we have the subscription book wholesale department, and in command of that department is Jimmy Ferguson,† who deserves great credit for his originality and persistent effort to sell books. He supplies the general agents, who in turn employ the men who go about with samples under their arms and sell to the customer. This business has grown with us to be quite an important branch, and Ferguson sells a great many books which are advertised by the mail-order department, thus gaining two markets from the same advertising.

Another department is Dan Nye's enterprise in selling to periodicals, which use the books as premiums. Both of these departments, I feel sure, are capable of more expansion in volume and great improvement in quality.

All these departments of bookselling are worthy of full attention and deepest study. Sometimes I think we rely too much on new books to carry our tremendous overhead. The good old standards which we have been selling for years offer many opportunities, and I am sure as time goes on we will avail ourselves of material which is bought and paid for and put away in the plate vaults; at least, let us hope so and strive to accomplish something new along these lines.

† James Ferguson left to form his own company which, many years later, became the Ferguson division of Doubleday & Company, Inc.

CHAPTER XLIV

OUR TWENTY-FIFTH
ANNIVERSARY

WHILE we are being grossly immodest, I will set down here a few words about a thing that gave me a great deal of pleasure and satisfaction.

In 1922 we celebrated the twenty-fifth anniversary of the founding of our business. We had a rather notable and interesting year. I was presented with a superbly printed and bound book signed by every member of the staff, and I copy here the kindly reference to me, which of course is not justified by the facts, but which gives me, probably, more pleasure on that account:

SILVER JUBILEE

DOUBLEDAY, PAGE & COMPANY

The year nineteen hundred and twenty-two is our year of great distinction. It is a year in which we shall present to the public both distinguished authors and fine specimens of book and magazine making. It also marks the twenty-fifth anniversary of the entrance of our leader and founder, Mr. F. N. Doubleday, into the publishing business.

Twenty-five years ago Mr. Doubleday, then in the employ of Charles Scribner's Sons, dreamed a dream of what a great publishing house should be. Practical idealist that he is and was, three years later he founded this business and set out to realize his ideal.

The great house which we serve to-day is the embodiment of our founder's ideal. That this embodiment, of which we are all so justly proud, is still far from realizing his vision, no one knows as well as he.

Conscious that much remains to be done, we, the undersigned, do hereby dedicate and rededicate ourselves, on this our founder's anniversary, to exert our utmost efforts to the end that we may, under his inspiring leadership, bring to pass the complete realization of his ideal.

In addition to this they gave me a beautiful old watch which Mrs. Williamson brought over from Bath, England, and which is one of my most cherished possessions.

I wish it were possible to take every member of the staff by the hand, and I wish, also, it were possible that I had the gift to communicate to them some appreciation of what this all means to me, but I am afraid this is beyond my limited powers.

CHAPTER XLV

NASSAU AND
MANCHESTER RANCHES

PROVIDENCE has had a busy time trying to protect me from my own impetuous folly. I always have been impetuous and very often have decided things too quickly, but somehow, by the grace of God, I have managed to pull through, and some of the most reckless things have turned out to be the pleasantest.

For instance, several years ago I met a man named Stratton, who had bought a point of land on the western end of the island of New Providence in the Bahamas, and he asked me to buy a piece of property and put up a house next door to him.

I told him that I would do so if Florence approved. He asked Florence and she did approve, and she then drew a plan for a house, and within a week workmen were on the job creating what afterwards became Jungle Cove House.

I did not get punished for this recklessness. Stratton, being a level-headed, quiet chap, waited until conditions should be perfect before attempting to build. The conditions are not perfect yet, and although three or four years have gone by, he still has no home in Nassau, whereas our house was finished in the unprecedented speed of one year and we have enjoyed its hospitality and had many friends with us for three winters.

Thus my impetuosity has resulted in a delightful experience. We have had many people come from the shop to spend a week or two; on the sands of the beach in front of Jungle Cove House all the affairs of the nations have been discussed over and over again; and we have settled a good many questions under a blazing sun which might have taken longer to settle in an ordinary winter snowstorm. I flatter myself that these friends have had a good time, especially the ones from the office.

Another occasion when I jumped before I thought was the purchase of the little farmhouse in Manchester, Vermont. We were visiting Mr. and Mrs. Bill Powers, who had bought a house in Manchester. They told us of a little farmhouse with one hundred acres of land which was on the market for five thousand dollars. They had thought of buying it for themselves, but had decided that it was too far from the hotel (three miles) for their children to be satisfied with it, and so had abandoned the idea. When they told me that it had a gigantic spring which fed the house with all the water it needed and made a brook of considerable proportions, we were fascinated with the idea, and on our way down to Albany and home we stopped and looked at this house, and more particularly at the brook and the spring.

When we got to Albany we telegraphed Bill Powers to

buy it, and after some delay we became possessed of what is now known as The Readery, a place where we can go and be quiet, and read and study and think.

Personally, I did not think the house was good enough to make over, but Florence, with her ingenuity and energy, as well as vision, re-created it and filled it full of antique furniture and various other things. It is seldom that she gets her hands on a house that she does not fill it full of antique furniture. She tells me that this is particularly beautiful American antique furniture; at all events, she got it at bargain-counter prices, which is really the important joy in buying antique furniture.

Both of these places have given us unalloyed pleasure. At Manchester we had a corn crib which was turned into a little guest room which sleeps two people very comfortably, with running water, etc.

From the door of Oyster Bay across the Sound to the door of The Readery is just two hundred miles, and we have done it many times without varying more than a mile or two. Unfortunately, of late we have not been able to spend much time there, but in the first year of the corn crib I think we had thirty-one visitors who at least spent the night. Here, again, as in Jungle Cove, many of the visitors were from the office, and under the apple trees we have settled many points, some of them I hope successfully—at all events, we still live and have three square meals a day.

I can only be thankful for the merciful Providence which lets me do foolish things and come out ahead of the game. Probably the most reckless thing that I did on a moment's inspiration was the buying of the Heinemann business, which I have described in the chapter devoted to that subject; but I should like to lay claim to having made that decision which, although it may have seemed reckless, was based on the solid principle of values. Of course it was lucky that Nelson was with me at the time; his faith in the success of Heinemann's greatly helped me to believe that we could run the necessary risk in the matter of a couple of hundred thousand dollars. So here, again, a kind Providence looked after us, with some slight assistance on our own part.

AN AFTERWORD

"EFFENDI"
FRANK NELSON DOUBLEDAY
1862 – 1934

by
Christopher Morley

EFFENDI (the nickname was Kipling's coinage, suggested, of course, by the initials) suited him perfectly. It had the quality of affectionate intimacy, but no one was likely to use it prematurely; and one did not forget that the word is a title of respect. All, whether editorial cubs or the most irreverent ink-stained printer in the pressroom, loved him for his humor, his easy masterful way, but respected him also with a little something of awe. The good old monosyllable big is the word that comes first to mind. He really was an effendi. In his office at Garden City there used to be a photograph of him taken in the burnous of an Arab chief. How well he looked the part: the tall, athletic figure, the bronzed face with its fine eagle nose, the brilliant eyes. It was always a thrill for us youngsters when we saw him coming into the office with his long swinging stride. One was instantly aware of power. The sound of the bindery machines on the floor below seemed to move with steadier rhythm; everything began to co-ordinate a little faster, a little smoother. People began going in and out of the big room in the corner, and there was an exciting feeling that things were doing. If I could just give you an impression of the strong, unhurried and yet unstoppable way he used to come down the aisle you would get some notion of the man. He seemed to gather speed and force (but never mere hurry) as he got near that corner room. He always came in as though some idea was urgent and motive in his mind, something he wanted to do promptly. I used to think what a grand experience it would be to serve as his secretary for a while, to get some idea of his extraordinary gift of easy, calm achievement, his genius for human relations. He was himself a writer of much humorous charm. There was once a little book called *A Plain American in England,* published as by "Charles T. Whitefield," which even many of his own staff did not know was by him. It was delightful, dwelling upon phases of Anglo-American comedy which always amused him. He, no less than his partner, Walter Page, was one of the most valuable ambassadors of friendship the two nations have ever had. His insistence on his own plainness, rusticity, was very characteristic of so subtle a negotiator.

It was touching to see, among the flowers at his funeral the other day, a large floral replica of a book—from one of the departments at the Country Life Press, I expect. There was a good simple symbolism about that, like the old workmen or warriors who were buried with their tools and weapons beside them. It was an afternoon of brilliant sunshine and snow, and after the service at the church it occurred to some of us to go over and look at the sun dial in the garden at the Press. Snow was crusted deep over it, but we rubbed it away; the bronze facsimiles of the old printers' marks were bright and clear. How surprised Aldus of Mantua would have been to find his own dolphin and anchor reprinted in that Long Island garden. And those of us who in one way or another had worked for Effendi and loved him couldn't help feeling that what would please him most would be for us to get back to town and sell some books.

His passionate enthusiasm for the job never failed even in the long years of illness. George Seiffert [a senior salesman at Doubleday] remembers how, long ago, he was hustling to catch a train back to the city after the weekly conference at the Press. Effendi met him in the aisle. "Selling any books, George?" George, caught unawares, and modestly embarrassed, took refuge in jocularity. "Once in a while," he said bashfully, and hastened on. Effendi called back. "Try all the while," he said.

Not only for his enthusiasm, for his organizing genius, but for his delicious humor The Boys loved him. There was a peculiar tenderness in the relation during these last years when the man we had known so strong, so unshakable, was broken down with long illness. Even then he would drive over to the Press every day; when he could no longer get out of the car members of the staff would go out to drive with him; his passion for every business detail never left him. During long drives he enjoyed dictating reminiscences of the various humors and crises of publishing. I wish I had available at this moment a copy of those *Indiscreet Recollections,* as he called them —a small book printed in only a few copies for his im-

mediate family. That, I remember telling him, was the
true Parnassus on Wheels, for it was composed entirely in
his famous Packard—which, he thriftily liked to remark,
had run over 140,000 miles. Shrewd sense about money
matters was strong in him as in all great men of affairs.
He never forgot, in telling the story of the time when he
and Sam McClure, a pair of young publishers, were offered the management of the famous Harper business,
that the excited McClure interrupted him in the middle of
a telephone call to Philadelphia which cost 75 cents.

Anecdotes of Effendi would be innumerable wherever
publishers, booksellers, or writers get together. Some of
those anecdotes would concern famous names, for he had
walked with greatness of many kinds. We used to think
secretly, we young zealots, of his renown, that in any
company anywhere Effendi would be at once recognizable
as extraordinary; and indeed it was so. Men of every sort
had always recognized him as someone to tie to. He had
hardly started his own business when President McKinley
wanted him to print a book of his speeches—a fine way
to lose money, and Effendi was shrewd enough to evade it.
John D. Rockefeller told him his life story during games
of golf. Andrew Carnegie advised him about his savings.
Frank Norris read manuscripts for him. Rudyard Kipling
wrote *Just So Stories* for Effendi's youngsters. (Doubleday
had slept on a couch in Kipling's sitting room at the
Grenoble Hotel when Kipling was desperately ill in New
York, so that he might not be disturbed.) A Prime Minister
of Great Britain has testified to the lasting impression
a meeting with Effendi made on him. Even while sitting
in the chair at an Imperial Conference, he confessed, he

found his thoughts wandering to a recollection of Frank Doubleday. But I am thinking now of the love and admiration he inspired in those who worked closest to him and who saw him in the full gusto of his power. He had also a delicious skill in pricking bubbles that needed bursting. I remember once, long ago, going in (after secret indignant brooding) to tell him that I really thought a raise in salary was disgracefully overdue. I had fermented the matter in private (it was very serious to me) until I was probably a bit incoherent, but he listened patiently. When there was an opportunity he asked how much I was getting. I told him. "Yes," he said blandly, "there must be something wrong if you haven't made yourself worth more than that." He must have passed on a good word, for a raise came through the next day, but the double significance of his comment remained memorable.

In his private office there was always a framed notice to the effect that a man can get a lot of good work done if he doesn't worry about who gets the credit for it. Lyman Stowe, another of his alumni, is reminded by this of a time when Effendi himself brought up some idea at the weekly editorial meeting. Everyone except Stowe was opposed to the suggestion. After the meeting Effendi called him in. "Stowe," he said, "you seemed to be the only one who thought there might be a glimmering of sense in that scheme. Suppose you wait about six weeks and then bring it up again as your own idea. Maybe then we can put it over."

There was an office episode Effendi enjoyed recalling, one which I often think of when I find myself buried rather deep in papers. A young man of whom Effendi was very fond, son of one of his North Shore neighbors, had a minor post in the Manufacturing Department which involved checking a great many orders, estimates, job schedules, etc. It so happened that the shortest path to Effendi's own office led past Billy P.'s desk, and Mr. Doubleday was always annoyed by the enormous mass of papers there. The Effendi was a great believer in cleaning up one's desk before going home, and finally he mentioned the matter. He did it in his usual oblique way: he took Billy into the private office, pointed to his own desk, which was clear of all debris, and remarked that that was what a desk should look like. But Billy, a young man of thoughtful disposition, always liked to rationalize everything with a little argument. "Yes, Mr. Doubleday," he said, "but you forget the volume of work that passes over my desk." One evening, Effendi, coming by after Billy had gone home, swept off all the floating papers, deposited them in a drawer in his own room, and waited to see what would happen. He claimed that everything went on just the same and Billy never knew the difference. . . .

Effendi was really the first of a new era in book publishing—which he visualized foremost as a business, not merely as a dignified literary avocation. He realized, perhaps more clearly than any other man, that the possibilities of book distribution have hardly been scratched. He developed the mail order and subscription phases of the business to remarkable dimensions. Against much opposition and advice he moved his business twenty miles out into the country to secure space and attractive working conditions; he repeated the same brilliantly successful experiment when he became majority owner of the famous

Heinemann imprint in England. He was inexhaustible in fertile schemes for larger distribution. The idea that publishing should be essentially an intelligently conducted commerce, not a form of aesthetic bohemianism, appealed strongly to his authors. He was, I think, the first publisher anywhere to submit to his authors royalty statements backed and substantiated by outside accountants. He developed a successful chain of his own bookstores as laboratories of selling. He was frequently under fire from the Trade for his experiments in new directions, but I think he firmly believed that every form of book distribution is ultimately a repercussion of benefit. No man was ever more enthusiastic in his heart for fine things; he dreamed night and day of a list which would be the greatest ever put together. When a group of de luxe French binders found the going too hard in New York he moved them bodily out to Garden City to do special jobs of beauty. Years ago, before the name of Joseph Conrad was known to more than a few critics, he was contributing a monthly stipend to keep Conrad writing—and this long before any of Conrad's books were under his own imprint. It was his young enthusiasm that first got all Stevenson's books together under the Scribner name. On his own list, to speak only of the greatest, there were three for whom his service can never be forgotten—Kipling, O. Henry, and Conrad. Those are his classics.

And now, as he would say when talk began to run overlong, let's get back to work.

P.S. I was late with this copy and was hastily reading it over as I came downtown in the subway. I looked up and

saw a girl carrying a book—a book that has the Doubleday
name on its back and which would never have been
written but for him. And that, I thought to myself, is the
great publisher's real epitaph. Many thousands, to whom
his name may mean little, yet carry it round with them. It
seemed symbolic of the endless way in which our trade,
though small in figures, interweaves human lives and can
even move the globe itself. It was that "dynamite and
wildcats" (a phrase of his own) which he felt in the publishing business, and in which he took more manly joy
than any man I have known.

Christopher Morley.

INDEX